Putting
God
In His
Place

Putting
God
In His
Place

Making Sure He Receives
the Worship He Deserves

DAVID MAINS
&
LAURIE MAINS

Star Song
PUBLISHING GROUP

PUTTING GOD IN HIS PLACE

Produced for Star Song by The Livingstone Corporation. Dr. James C. Galvin, Michael Kendrick, and Brenda James Todd, project staff.

ISBN 1-56233-252-X

Printed in the United States of America

3 4 5 6 7 8 9 Printing/Year 99 98 97 96 95 94

Dedicated to John and Bette Stocks
for guiding me (Laurie)
in my first steps down the path of worship
and for encouraging my (David's)
daughter-in-law to find
her greatest delight in the Lord.

Contents

Foreword

After I read this book, *Putting God In His Place*, by David Mains and his daughter-in-law Laurie, my mind wandered back to an incident that occurred in a classroom in Wheaton College in 1982.

I was teaching a course on worship and was strongly emphasizing the need to recover worship in the evangelical community. When class was over a very thoughtful young man came to me and said, "You know you're wasting your time, don't you?"

"What do you mean?" I answered in what I'm sure was a highly surprised tone of voice.

"Worship, you know."

"No, I don't know. What are you talking about?"

"Worship. You are too focused on the subject and you are going to wind up wasting your whole life because of your enthusiasm for it."

"How so?" I asked with a strong dose of curiosity mixed with a Who-do-you-think-you-are-to-tell-me-I'm-wasting-my-life attitude.

"It's no use."

"What's no use?"

"Teaching and writing about worship."

"What?"

"Yeah! It's a waste of your energy, your time, your life. No one is interested! Besides you are working against four hundred years of neglect. Protestants, and particularly evangelicals, don't care. And they never will. So why bother? Find something else to be committed to."

I've never forgotten that conversation. And while this student was right about the four hundred years of neglect, he's wrong about wasting time on worship.

This is why I am so heartened by this book, *Putting God In His Place*, and by the interest of so many evangelicals all over the country in the subject of worship. The Holy Spirit is awakening the church to its primary duty in worship.

In this book, David and Laurie introduce four themes of worship chosen for the annual Worship Celebration, 1994. And in a most interesting and anecdotal way they lead us into four very central issues of worship—that we are the people of praise, the people of the event, the people of celebration, and the people of service—and they do so in a way that is faithful to the biblical and historical tradition of Christian worship.

Worship is all about God and our relationship to him. In worship we rehearse this relationship and find our spiritual lives strengthened and nourished again and again. Read this book and find out more about how your relationship with God is established, sustained, repaired, and transformed through worship.

Robert E. Webber
Professor of Theology
Wheaton College
and Director, Institute for Worship Studies

My Compliments
to the King

People of praise attribute worth to God through laudatory words.

In your imagination, picture an endless row of continuous-feed computer paper. Poke a pinhole in the first sheet. That represents our earth, which is eight thousand miles in diameter. Five-eighths of an inch away, put a speck for the moon. Twenty pages further, cut a two-inch ball for the sun. Mars will require thirty-two more sheets of paper. Six hundred fifty pages from the sun you can include Neptune. But how far do you think you have to go beyond the pinhole to include the nearest star? Astronomers tell us you will need to travel over a thousand miles! That's approximately from where we live in Chicago all the way to Denver.

As a father and daughter-in-law, we are grappling with the concept of worship. What does it mean to attribute worth to the God who made the universe? Is it simply a feeling we get when we're in church? Or is it action that touches the whole of our lives? And if it *is* an action, how do we *do* it?

To *worship* means "to attribute worth to God." Another way of stating this is that we're letting our Lord know how important he is to us. We're allowing Christ to take his rightful place as King

11

of our lives.

When we titled this book *Putting God in His Place,* some people questioned our word choice. "Sounds like you're putting him down," they cautioned. But we're hoping the title grabbed your attention. Without the subtitle, *Making Sure He Receives the Worship He Deserves,* maybe it appears as if we're shaking our finger at God and admonishing him for being too big for his britches. But that's not the way it is at all. If there's any finger-pointing to be done, it's in our direction for failing to put God in his rightful place. We know he has to be first in the lives of his subjects. And we believe we have learned some elementary ways to make that evident to him—to attribute worth to God. We'd like to share them with you in these four chapters.

When thinking about worshipping God, the first concept that pops into most people's heads is praise. Worship isn't limited to praise, but that's a good beginning place for understanding what it is all about. *Praise* is putting into appropriate words what we appreciate about our Master.

Do you like it when somebody pays you a compliment? Of course you do. In one sense, learning to praise is learning to pay God a compliment. So one obvious way we can worship God is by telling him how wonderful and how important he is to us.

It seems simple, doesn't it? But then, why do we find it so hard to come up with words to praise God? "God, you're great. God, you're . . . um . . .

12

great." Do you ever fall into that trap? Later on in this chapter, we'll suggest how you can develop your praise life. But let's begin by looking up at the grandeur of our King and reminding ourselves of some of the reasons why he's so deserving of our praise.

The Greatest of Kings

Hebrews chapter 1 declares, "[God] has spoken to us by his Son, whom he appointed heir of all things, and through whom he made the universe. The Son is the radiance of God's glory and the exact representation of his being, sustaining all things by his powerful word." That verse holds some mind-boggling truths that relate to why we praise the Lord.

He is King of the universe. Astronomy measures distances in light years. That's the distance light will travel in a year at the speed of 186,000 miles per second. (That may be downhill all the way, but it's still making good time!) In the course of a year, that amounts to six trillion miles. That's difficult to comprehend, so think of it this way: A bullet shot at the speed of light would circle the earth and hit you in the back seven times before you could fall—even if it only took you one second to fall.

At the speed of light, you could go from Los Angeles to New York in one-sixtieth of a second. You would pass the moon one and three-sixteenths seconds later. You would reach the sun in eight minutes, traverse the entire solar system in eleven hours, and arrive at the nearest star in four and three-tenths years. But to get to the North Star it would take four hundred long years. To cross the Milky Way would require one hundred thousand years, and it's estimated that outer space contains (hold on!) over a hundred million galaxies like our Milky Way, each with billions of stars. No wonder astronomy textbooks state that there are more heavenly bodies the size of the Earth or larger than there are grains of sand upon our planet!

We landed a man on that speck five-eighths of an inch from the little pinhole on our computer paper and sometimes fancy we hold the scepter that rules the universe. But that's not so. Keep in mind the verse referred to earlier, which reads: "He has spoken to us by his Son, *whom he appointed heir of all things, and through whom he made the universe*" (italics ours). We praise our Lord for his incomprehensible creative power.

He is King of our bodies. While David enjoys studying astronomy, I (Laurie) have never been too interested in stars—except when I'm feeling romantic. From my grade school years until I was seventeen, I wanted to be a nurse. So I paid close attention to what I was taught about the human body. Colossians 1 reads, "For by him *all* things were created." According to Genesis, the crowning achievement of the Originator was his creation of humankind. And if nothing is written about the mind or the personality or the breath of life that makes us unique spiritual beings, and if only the physical body is referred to, Christ's handiwork still flabbergasts me.

Science tells me there are a thousand miles of blood vessels in my body, and one million, five hundred thousand sweat glands on its surface. My lungs are composed of seven hundred million cells. If my heartbeats for this single day were constricted into one throb of vital power, it would be sufficient to throw a ton of iron one hundred twenty feet into the air.

My nervous system is controlled by a brain that has three trillion nerve cells, of which nine billion, two hundred million are in the cortex, or covering of the brain, alone. If in my veins there are three million white corpuscles and one hundred eighty trillion (that's 180,000,000,000,000) red ones, I can't help but think the great complexity of my body must be the work of someone with unsurpassed wisdom and creativity. That's quite a reason to praise him!

Being Subjects of the King

What's important is that we understand we're referring to someone who is unique. There is no one else like Christ. He is not our peer. Nobody even begins to compare with this King to whom we are subject. The Hebrews 1 passage discloses that when Christ "had provided purification for sins, he sat down at the right hand of the Majesty in heaven." This is a monarch who doesn't just sit on the throne of some nation; Christ sits at the right hand of the very majesty of God on high. We'll come back to the concept of providing purification for sins. But when we consider glorifying Jesus, or lauding him, or upholding his name, we obviously aren't capable of doing this to the degree he deserves. Still, it's imperative that we try.

"Why attempt something so impossible?" you may ask. The answer is that as subjects of this greatest of all kings, it is fitting that we do so.

We are his subjects because he has authority over us. God is much bigger than the tiny world we experience, so all illustrations break down in one way or another. But see if this example helps clarify why we worship Christ.

I (David) have never been in the court of any actual king. In fact, the only court I've been in is traffic court. Even in that setting, however, when the judge came in, the clerk called out, "All rise!" Naturally, I stood up, as did everyone else in the room. I would have been foolish not to. I did this because it was the appropriate thing to do for someone who had the power to decide a small part of my future. The office demanded my respect.

In a similar way, isn't it proper for me to pay homage to the Son of God, who holds my entire life in his hands? His office of King of the universe claims far more reverence than I know how to give. And yet I must do my best to act properly.

We are his subjects because of his great love for us. Before Christ became our King, we were subjects of Satan. We were afraid of him, but we didn't spend time trying to put into words the respect we had for his power or authority. We didn't pay him heart-felt compliments because he didn't deserve them—he definitely didn't treat us in a loving fashion.

But this new King who originally made the universe and all that is in it—and who created us to know him and love him—has now, through his death and resurrection, reconciled us to himself. That's what Paul writes in Colossians chapter 1, that Christ has made peace through his blood shed on the cross. We who have experienced this incredible love can't keep from praising him.

In other words, the very hands that spun the universe into existence had to writhe with pain from nails that pierced them. The head crowned with majesty at the right hand of God once wore a crown of thorns. And why is this? Because of his great concern for us, and because of our need for someone to provide purification for our sins. The song "How Great Thou Art" expresses it so well. After the magnificent verses about the beauty of creation, the hymnist declares:

> And when I think that God, his Son not sparing
> Sent him to die, I scarce can take it in!
> That on the cross, my burden gladly bearing
> He bled and died to take away my sin.
> Then sings my soul, my Savior God to Thee,
> How great Thou art, how great Thou art!

How Subjects Act

When a subject approaches a king, he or she doesn't say, "How are you, anyway? Have you had a tough day, Big Guy?" No. Instead, you come into the court of a monarch expecting first to bow. This body position immediately indicates, "I am the subject, you are the ruler. You are the one with authority, you are more important than I am. It is my privilege to be here at your invitation."

And you plan to use your best words to pay him the finest compliments you can.

For Americans who don't live in that kind of world, try viewing things this way: If you were to see the president while you were out jogging, you wouldn't say, "How're you doin', babe?" unless you wanted to be seen as having the maturity level of some uninformed junior high schooler. Rather, you would say, "Good morning, Mr. President." Here again, the office demands a certain respect. If you violate that protocol, you have acted in a way that's highly improper.

Maybe you've seen the movie *In the Line of Fire*. Toward the beginning of the film, the character played by John Malcovich telephones Secret Service agent Clint Eastwood and says he's going to kill the president. Eastwood counters, "It's a federal offense to threaten the president, even if you're only joking." To joke like this is a crime because it trivializes the presidential office. So too, we offend Christ when we trivialize his status in our lives. The truth is, if we don't know how to praise our King, we belittle him. Considering who he is and who we are, this should not be the case.

Worship on Sundays

The church has always taken seriously how Christ's subjects are to act in worship. And it's important that parishioners come to services with the awareness that the King is actually going to be there. He may not be there bodily, but he will literally be there through his Spirit. What we want to do is act the same way we would if we saw

Christ dressed in royalty and holding out to us his hands that were marred in our behalf.

If Jesus were to bodily attend your church this Sunday, how would people act? Probably their first response would be in worship. Many would bow. Others might prostrate themselves before him. Some might look into his eyes in adoration. This is the body language of worship. And if subjects dared say anything, they would first speak complimentary words of praise. That's what you'd expect.

It thrills us that praise is sweeping today's church. Believers are sensing the presence of the Lord on Sundays in a new and marvelous way. Many are actually coming to services early in order to have more time to worship their King. The music of worship is taking on new expressions. And Christians are delighting in singing praises to their Lord. Tears are not all that uncommon in services. Put succinctly, the church is experiencing a new day of praise.

We are blessed with his presence. Suppose you said to a fellow-worker, "I wrote a song about your many good qualities, and ten people have rehearsed it. They want to sing it for you—will you come and listen?" You'd hope that person would respond, "Of course. I wouldn't miss it for anything!"

The church is not in a make-believe position. In church, we declare, "Christ, we trust you're going to be with us when we gather on Sunday morning. So we have rehearsed in order to express to the best of our ability the praise we feel you deserve. Our choir and congregation have gone out of their way to put into proper words our adoration both in song and in prayer. We will come to your house with the desire to hear you speak to us, but we will also arrive with the intention of telling you how much we appreciate you. Even if we hear nothing new from you, we will leave the service satisfied if we can laud you in a way that reveals where our hearts are."

What we are writing about is not whether you like praise songs or the old hymns of the faith. It isn't a matter of lifting hands or sitting and quietly bowing your head. It's first a question of whether your congregation understands the phenomenal privilege it has of Christ being present whenever two or three gather in his name. Next, when we're convinced he is truly there, is it our earnest desire to praise him to the best of our ability?

Therefore, our attitude in his church must praise him. For too many worshippers it's not a big thing to come to a service late. Understand, however, that Christ is present—at the very beginning of most services there is a call to worship, or to attribute worth to him. This is meant to help prepare everyone for what is to happen. It almost seems like an offense to be habitually unpunctual.

To come in tired because you stayed up to watch "Saturday Night Live," or to come hungry because you were in a hurry and skipped breakfast, is to act foolishly toward a great privilege you have been given. We need, instead, to consider the magnitude of the opportunity at hand and to come as prepared as we can possibly be. His Majesty the King is to be in church today. Jesus, the one who touched our lives and made them better, will be in attendance. He is giving us an opportunity to say how grateful we are. Ours is the unique advantage of participating in what the body of Christ has known down through the ages—we share in the continuing privilege of being people of praise.

If everyone would come to church on Sunday with a great desire to praise the Lord, it would be a huge step forward in the church. We believe this is beginning to happen. More and more, God's people are understanding the honor he has bestowed upon them, and they are finding great delight in expressing their praise to the Lord.

Picture them in all different kinds of church settings. In some, the believers stand with hands uplifted, tears streaming down their cheeks, and voices raised in praise. In others, they bow their heads quietly before the symbol of the cross, but their emotion is just as intense. Some congregations use prayer books and hymnals. Others sing praise choruses with the use of an overhead projector. In certain sanctuaries they enter with banners; in others they dance. The instruments vary from organ to guitar, drums to strings. All in all, this is a marvelous new day.

Worship Every Day

Even so, we feel there is another major step church people must take. It's not enough to be involved in praise one day along with everyone else in the corporate body. Praise also needs to be infused into each of our daily lives. Christians aren't doing as well here. We're optimistic that we'll begin to see some changes in this area, just like the ones we're observing in so many of our church services.

Frankly, it's easier to enter into the praise of the Lord in a corporate setting. We get caught up with the closeness of others. We draw on the great hymn and chorus writers who have done such a good job of putting into words what we want to express. But it's different when you're all alone. A college dorm room or a second-floor flat is not as advantageous a place to feel the presence of the Lord.

Before I (Laurie) got married I lived by myself in a studio apartment, and I had an upstairs neighbor who was aspiring to be a rock singer. He would practice his guitar and wail out strange songs at the most inopportune times. Often, it was just when I was winding down for the night, trying to focus my thoughts on the Lord and giving myself over to him. I found it hard to concentrate on God when "Elvis"—as I used to call him—was bellowing above!

Are your children sometimes a distraction for you? Maybe you find yourself worrying about all the odd jobs you need to do. Or possibly the television, the computer, even the briefcase still pose as competition to your individual praise of the One who made the world and all that's in it. You may find you need to plan your praise time around your kids' nap or homework times. Shutting off the TV or computer, closing the briefcase, taking the phone off the hook—

determinedly tearing yourself away from anything that competes for your attention—doing this in order to spend time complimenting the Lord attributes worth to him. What a wonderful example of worship!

Praise is a marvelous tool for each day. I (Laurie) must admit that I'm not an expert at praising God on my own time. I've had the opportunity to learn so much from David as we've been working on this book. One evening I sat down to "pick his brain," and I'd like to share our conversation with you.

L: David, I agree that we need to learn to praise God every day, but I'm having trouble figuring out how to do that! Part of it may be my attitude of submission to the King as his subject, but aren't there some specific actions I can take that will help me praise him?

D: Of course! Some easy ways to do this would include purchasing a hymnal of your own and think-ing through the lyrics as you read a few each day. Then when you come to church you're able to sing the various songs with much more mean-ing—it's not the first time you've seen them. Another way, obviously, is to memorize Scripture. Go through what you learn about God in a given verse and then tell the Lord, "It says here that you curse the wicked, but you bless the righteous. I'm going to affirm this about you, because the day will come when I'll need to have it locked in my mind that you are just. Even though the world doesn't always seem just to me, I know you are just and fair because that's what's taught in this Scripture about you."

L: So I should plan to praise God when I read my Bible?

D: Sure, but you can also praise God at other times. You might spontaneously find yourself praising him for some aspect of himself. You'd say, almost after the fact, "It's really neat what you did today, God. You certainly have a funny sense of humor—it was amazing to me how you took care of me! I had to laugh because you came in with an answer right out of left field! I would never have figured out a solution like you did. You always know what you're doing, don't you?"

L: Maybe I'd notice God's sense of humor through something I read in the Bible—for instance, Sarah being pregnant at age 90—

D: Yeah, that's a funny picture, isn't it? A pregnant old lady, who's never had a child, walking around happy as a lark and big as a barn!

L: —Or I'd commend God for something funny he did during my day—like when my windshield wiper wasn't working and he made the crazy snowflakes fall everywhere on my car except the one spot I needed to be able to see!

D: You know, I try to keep a list of things I know about God that people don't normally think about. For example, you seldom hear a praise song about how God is a great communicator, or how our Lord is extremely personal, but he is! I'm convinced he knows my needs even before they come up. That's another one. Try to think of a song about how God is full of surprises. Where have you ever seen a hymn like that?

L: I'd love to write a song about how God enjoys the look on our faces when he comes up with one of his slam-bang surprises!

D: That's right! And it's too bad we never sing about God being so adept at last-minute rescues, but I sense that's one of his specialties. Sometimes when I'm in a fix I just say, "Well, this is very typically God—he's lasting this thing out to the very end. I believe he's got this sense of the dramatic, but he's going to come through! Just wait and see!"

L: Is there any other way I can practice praise during the week besides thinking of what God is and telling him about how I appreciate it?

D: Part of your answer may be as simple as getting a praise tape for the car and listening to that instead of The Chapel of the Air. When you mentally track with it—

L: Wait a minute. Instead of The Chapel??

D: Okay, I take it back! But at other times I can listen to Johnny Mathis (that dates me) or I can pop in a George Gershwin cassette, or I can listen to a praise tape. I make a choice. It's as simple as that. As far as that goes, you can read books about praise. There are lots of them. A person who's poor at praise can go to the local Christian bookstore and find any number of titles on the topic.

L: And reading about how to praise is actually

an act of worship?

D: Could be, because you're saying to God, "You are most important in my life, and I'm choosing to learn how to express that." And if the book's a good one, you'll soon come away praising! You see, Laurie, praise is not all that complicated. I do it all the time, and so can you.

I'm learning that David is right, and I hope you will come to the same conclusion.

Praise him for what he'll do today. Another way we can incorporate praise into the everyday is by figuring out what attribute of God we need for the day. For instance, you might say, "Lord, I've got a schedule today that would choke a horse. But you are eternal, and you can touch my day with eternity so that when it's over, it looks like I got three days' work done."

Or, you might pray, "Lord, you are my shield and my defender. I've got a guy who's going to disrupt my day today because he's a known pain in the neck." That "pain" may be an employee or an employer or an acquaintance, but you can pray, "God, I need you to block him out, just like a linebacker, so when he starts to tackle me—bam!— you knock his lights out. If I find you've done that in a way I didn't even think about, I'm going to praise you. Believe me, I will!"

In fact, I (David) love to take on a problem in my early morning prayers. I'll say, "God, this is your problem. I'm rather eager to see how you'll figure out a solution. I know you're wise, I know you have incredibly creative skills, I know you have all the wealth in the world. My problem is not really a problem to you. So please play those many attributes of yours in concert and see how things come about. Okay? Thank you!"

Praise him through "Majesty Memoirs." Maybe, like me (Laurie), you worry that you'll end up praying for what you need more than praising God for how he is powerful enough to supply that need. Here's another daily way of approaching the same "application-style" praise. Lately I've been keeping a list of every attribute I'm learning about God in my Scripture reading. David has filled an entire three-ring binder full of characteristics of God, and when he showed it to me, I began doing the same thing.

I followed David's format in setting up my "Majesty Memoirs," as I've named them. When I come across a new characteristic of God in my reading, I begin a new entry. Then I write down the address of the verse in which I found that trait. In parentheses I indicate briefly how it's used. Underneath all this I write any notes I might find helpful about what the entry word means or how it might help me in my life.

David keeps all of his entries on loose-leaf notebook paper, so he can alphabetize them in his three-ring binder. (I haven't managed to get that organized yet!) Here's a sample page from his notebook on the Psalms:

> *Abhorrer*   Ps. 106:40 (and he abhorred his heritage)
> loathe--to move away from in disgust

Acquitter	Ps. 69:27 (may they have no acquittal from thee)
	a setting free, being declared not guilty
	close to the word JUDGE or ADVOCATE—See Trinity hymnal 222–223.
All-seeing	Ps. 10:14 (thou dost see; yea, thou dost note trouble and vexation)
	Ps. 11:4 (his eyes behold; his eyelids test, the children of men)
	Ps. 69:5 (the wrongs I have done are not hidden from thee)
	Ps. 115:12 (the Lord has been mindful of us)
	See Trinity hymnal 48.
Almighty	Ps. 68:14 (when the Almighty scattered kings there), etc.

As I (Laurie) write down what I'm learning about God's attributes in my reading of Genesis, I praise him for who he is. For instance, I might say, "Lord, it says here in Genesis 2:8 that you are a gardener. That's wonderful, because I love gardening! How much more breathtaking your Garden of Eden must have been compared to anything I could possibly cultivate. I praise you for the varieties of flowers and trees you made back then, and I can hardly believe how you keep producing them each year. Please allow me to understand what it means for you to be a gardener, and let me care for my own plants with the dedication I see in your care for yours."

It's surprising how what you read about God so often applies to the very day you'll be facing. That's when David's praise for the way God can solve his imminent problems becomes all the more real. If you were an artist, you might begin with the passage in Genesis that says God's work was creating. Then say to him, "God, this is such a good reminder to me—you're my awesome Creator, and you weren't just playing around when you made the universe. It was the work you had set for yourself. This is something I appreciate about you—you don't think imagination is foolish. I'm going to need to be creative in my own work today, so would you be so kind as to grant me some of your own imaginative abilities?"

The words are humble, but that's usually the way it is. You don't have to use hymn-quality phrases to praise God. You don't have to sound eloquent. We've found that the more we explore the ways we can praise God, the more impossible the job is. But that's good because it only means we're experiencing God as increasingly wonderful. And we hope you will join us in seeing him that way.

The truth is, if we try to plummet the depths of who God is, our spiritual jaws drop and we end up saying, "My Lord, this is incredible that you're even open to hearing my stumbling, bumbling praise. You're so great and you deserve infinitely more. But this is the best I can do. Please accept that my worship is from my heart and that I'm finding pleasure in bringing it to you."

In fact, if we were to turn over our continuous-feed computer paper, on which we outlined a tiny partial model of the solar system and the nearest star, we could use it in another way. We could write on each page something we know about God and the reasons we appreciate that quality.

And as we progressed to the next page, and the next, and the next, we'd explore God more and more, and we'd eventually realize that this exercise was going to stretch all the way from here to Denver. And outrageously enough, when it got to Colorado, that would be nothing! It could go on forever and ever. Because that's how great our King is. And that's why we praise him corporately on Sunday, but on our own with laudatory words every other day as well.

For Discussion and Reflection

1. Name a time when you appreciated the praise of someone else. How did that make you feel?

2. Give several reason why God deserves your praise.

3. What are some simple ways you could improve your Sunday praise?

4. What would be the easiest time for you to fit praise into your week days? What steps can you take to do this?

5. What is the difference between worship and praise? How might you illustrate this to a new believer?

6. If you have stopped thinking about how great the Lord is, what might you do to bring yourself back to reality?

Readings

Then there is *admiration*, that is, appreciation of the excellency of God. Man is better qualified to appreciate God than any other creature because he was made in his image and is the only creature who was. This admiration for God grows and grows until it fills our heart with wonder and delight. "In our astonished reverence we confess Thine uncreated loveliness," said the hymn writer. "In our astonished reverence." The God of the modern evangelical rarely astonishes anybody. He manages to stay pretty much within the constitution. Never breaks over our bylaws. He's a very well-behaved God and very denominational and very much one of us, and we ask Him to help us when we're in trouble and look to Him to watch over us when we're asleep. The God of the modern evangelical isn't a God I could have much respect for. But when the Holy Gost shows us God as He is we admire Him to the point of wonder and delight.

(A. W. Tozer, *Worship: The Missing Jewel of the Evangelical Church* [Camp Hill, Pa.: Christian Publications, 1979], pp. 26–27)

●●●●●●

Years ago, when I lived at home with my parents, one of the houses we lived in (we lived in them one at a time I hasten to add!) had what is a common feature of many houses. On an outside wall, about twelve feet up and projecting over a concrete path, was a pipe. Attached to this pipe on the inside of the house was a bath, and this particular pipe was connected to a little hole just beneath the taps, called an overflow. This overflow hole and its connecting pipe were a dead giveaway if any of us children had, in the pursuit of swimming experience, overfilled the bath, and our guilt was yet more explicitly revealed should one of our parents or a visitor walk on the path beneath the pipe just as somebody was practising a belly-flop! Praise and worship are the overflow of a life that is filled with God, and to carry the illustration over to our bodies for a moment, our overflow hole is situated just under the nose!

(Graham Kendrick, *Learning to Worship As a Way of Life* [Minneapolis: Bethany House, 1984], pp. 82–83)

●●●●●●

Justin tells us the congregation stood for prayer. Other sources tell us about the significance of this posture: A person kneeled or prostrated himself to express humility, contrition, repentance, confession of sin. Standing, on the other hand, was a sign of joy and boldness, showing the freedom of God's children to come boldly into his presence.

On the first day of the week, standing had a special reference also to the Resurrection. This was the characteristic Christian attitude in prayer, as other texts and archaeological findings confirm. For early Christians, standing meant one had special privileges to come to God as Father, through Christ. To stand in the presence of God meant to be accepted by him and to have the right to speak freely.

The prayer referred to at this point in the assembly was the corporate or common prayer. It was evidently a free prayer. Justin may give some idea of the typical content earlier in his *Apology:*

"We praise the Maker of the universe as much as we are able by the word of prayer and thanksgiving for all the things with which we are supplied.... Being thankful in word, we send up to him honors and hymns for our coming into existence, for all the means of health, for the various qualities of the different classes of things, and for the changes of the seasons, while making petitions for our coming into existence again in incorruption by reason of faith in him."

This summary statement accords with the general pattern that is found elsewhere: it begins with an address to God as Father and Creator, praises him for his mighty acts, moves from thanksgiving to petition, and closes with a doxology—all being done with reference to Christ.

("How We Christians Worship," by Justin Martyr translation and commentary by Everett Ferguson, *Christian History* 12:1 [1993]:13)

●●●●●●

These Saturday exercises are designed to begin the worshiping process in your heart so that you don't walk into your Sunday service needing to begin the work of worship "cold." Some churches pick a worship theme for each week, or a pastor may be working through a book of the Bible or a topical study. If you are able to discover ahead of time what these themes will be, integrate them into these activities.

Choose one exercise each week. They take very little time and are surprisingly effective in beginning the worship process in the heart.

Check one box each Saturday to show you have completed the assignment of your choice. Ten assignments are provided from which to choose.

☐ Write a short letter to God, as you might write to a friend. Express how, as you walk with God, you see that he is characterized by a certain attribute. In essence, this will be a written prayer. When you finish the letter, read it aloud to God.

☐ Set aside fifteen minutes on Saturday for a time of private adoration. Think about God. If you are praising him as all powerful, you may see him seated on a throne. If you are praising him for his love, you might imagine Christ on the cross. Then choose a posture appropriate for this mental picture: sitting, kneeling, walking together, etc. Once you have done this, tell Christ how pleased you are that he is characterized by the worship theme of that given Sunday.

☐ Choose a song that expresses your praise to God regarding worship. Through meditation, allow this music to capture your heart today.

☐ Think about God's work in your life. What has God proven himself to be for you? Now share your thoughts with someone else. Complete this exercise by thanking the Lord for the privilege of telling another of his worth.

☐ Look for a passage of Scripture that underscores a worship theme. You might want to choose verses from several parts of the Bible, much like you would if you were preparing a responsive reading. Tell God, "These verses are FROM you, but I also read them TO you." Then read them out loud to the Lord. You might do this as a prayer for your Saturday evening meal.

☐ The Psalmist often affirms God by reviewing how He worked in the past. Spend time looking back on your life. How has the Lord already proven himself to you? Write down on a sheet of paper at least five personal incidents that convince you he is worthy of your praise tomorrow.

☐ Spend fifteen minutes talking with a friend or family member about the Lord. Welcome Christ into your conversation as you remember his promise to be present when even two or three have gotten together in his name. Discuss together how Christ has proven himself in your lives.

☐ Poetry has often been used by God's people to express their adoration and praise. If you are gifted in this way, write something original. If not, find a poem that reflects a worship theme. Take the poem with you to church to silently read to the Lord in the quiet before the service.

☐ Adoration can sometimes be shown through gifts given to the Lord or to someone else on his behalf. In such a case one's prayer is: "Lord, this special gift is given as a way of expressing my praise to you. Accept it, I pray, as from the heart of one who loves you. Amen."

☐ Come up with an original way to express

praise to God as you prepare yourself for church tomorrow.

(Karen Burton Mains, *Making Sunday Special* [Nashville: Star Song, 1994], pp. 94-95)

••••••

Praise the LORD.
Praise God in his sanctuary;
  praise him for his mighty heavens.
Praise him for his acts of power;
  praise him for his surpassing greatness.
Praise him with the sounding of the
  trumpet,
  praise him with the harp and lyre,
  praise him with tambourine and dancing,
  praise him with the strings and flute,
  praise him with the clash of cymbals,
  praise him with resounding cymbals.
Let everything that has breath praise the
  LORD.
Praise the LORD.
(Psalm 150)

The Greatest Thing
That Ever Happened

People of the event attribute worth to God by making Christ central to how they live.

The owner of a mom-and-pop store in Los Angeles stared in disbelief as rioters, reacting to the Rodney King verdict, destroyed everything he and his family had worked for in the previous twelve years. A woman whose husband's helicopter was shot down over Vietnam grimly tackled life on her own, haunted by fears that he survived but was wasting away in a POW camp. A young Midwest couple dejectedly retreated to a shelter for the homeless as massive flooding devastated the farm on which they had spent their life savings.

Events shape our lives, sometimes in an extremely negative manner. There's no doubt about that.

But events can also affect people positively. At Christmas the Discover Card company encourages people to use their charge card by offering a contest in which someone will win a huge sum of money. The more you charge, the more often your name is entered into the drawing. Suppose you were the individual notified at the end of December that you had won their multimillion-dollar sweepstakes? You were just doing your regular Christmas shopping, using your Discover Card every so often—and now, suddenly, you're a millionaire. Think how your life would change: You could pay off all your bills, and then be as generous to others as you've always wanted to be. You might be able to finance a new church building for your home congregation, or maybe you could help out some unfortunate person left destitute after an earthquake or tornado. It would be safe to say this event had a most positive effect on your life!

"Getting religion" is another event that can have a phenomenal impact. Take, for example, civil rights leader Malcolm X. Before he became a Muslim, Malcolm got into a lot of trouble—so much that he ended up in jail. But while in prison he embraced Islam, and that event turned him entirely around. Morality, discipline, and knowledge began to accentuate his life. We disagree with his beliefs, but the discipline he learned made him quite a leader in the African-American community.

What Are People of the Event?

Certain events can go beyond shaping individual circumstances. Some are of such magnitude they affect the lives of vast multitudes. In the Bible there are two blockbuster events that influenced the people of the Old and New Testaments.

The first, and lesser of the two, is the Exodus event. Captive under an evil Pharaoh, the Hebrews were in dire need of a deliverer. Scripture describes how God brought the Israelites out of their bondage, led them through the desert, and eventually took them into the Promised Land, Canaan. This Exodus event takes precedence over everything else that happened. It established the Jews as a free nation and proclaimed to the world that the children of Israel were special to God.

The Exodus event was not just important because of its historical significance. The Lord himself said it was to be remembered throughout all succeeding generations, and he established the Passover feast to help his people remember what he did for them. That's why Jewish people make sure each child understands the meaning behind the Passover meal. "We were Pharaoh's slaves in Egypt," they say, "and the Lord our God rescued us with a mighty hand and an outstretched arm." They go on to explain that unleavened bread is eaten because "there was not enough time for our fathers' dough to rise." Bitter herbs are served because "the Egyptians made the lives of our fathers in Egypt so bitter and miserable." If you took the Exodus event out of a devout Jew's history, his or her whole life would change. That's why we call the Jews "people of the Exodus event."

In the New Testament, the Christ event is set above everything else. The Gospels tell us about something that changed far more than the development of a small nation. We'll call this happening, which altered our entire world, the *Christ event*—the virgin birth of Jesus, his powerful ministry to all people, his cruel death as a substitute for what we deserve, his miraculous resurrection, and his ascension in glory to the right hand of the Father. Nothing—no extraordinary incident of the past, no present-day news flash, no highly-imaginative story— will ever compare to this event.

Just as the Exodus event distinguishes Israel, the Christ event sets Christians apart as God's own. The Jews would be missing an essential part of worship without the story of the Exodus; similarly, the Christ event is integral to the lives of Christians. To overlook the Incarnation, to let it grow old, to allow something to replace it, would be a highly consequential error.

When God acts in a marvelous fashion, he wants us to pay attention. What can impact our way of living more than this: that God loved us so much he was willing to give up his only Son to make possible our salvation from Satan, the worst of tyrants? How can we help but worship our King in light of this sacrificial event?

Worshipping as People of the Event

In chapter one we said that worship means to attribute worth to God. We can do this by praising or complimenting him. I (David) can attribute worth to my wife Karen by telling her things I like about her.

• I'm pleased with what an excellent mother she has been to our four children.

• I like her positive attitude, and I really enjoy her distinctive laugh.

Saying what I (Laurie) like about Joel is easy, too.

• He knows how to act around people—put him in a group, and he really shines!

• He is an outstanding critic; his great creativity and constructive reasoning gently push me to improve.

Do our mates like it when we say positive things to them? You bet! Everyone appreciates a sincere compliment. We learned that in chapter one.

But through the years I (David) have also brought Karen pain by my actions. I am a recovering workaholic. I remember Karen telling me that my actions often spoke to her louder than my words did. I was better at *saying* I loved her than I was at *showing* it to her.

That's because far too often I spent inappropriate amounts of time at the office, and I even brought my work home and paid more attention to it than to my wife. "You never had a person who was a mistress," Karen once told me, "but maybe that would have been easier. At least I could have tried to compete. But how do you fight for attention against a never-ending ministry schedule that calls to your husband day in and day out?"

The Lord understands only too well this human tendency to get involved in secondary priorities and forget what's really important. That's why he clearly outlined to his people how they should always keep in mind the amazing things he did for them. For example:

> Do not eat . . . bread made with yeast, but for
> seven days eat unleavened bread, the bread of af-
> fliction, because you left Egypt in haste—so that
> all the days of your life you may remember the
> time of your departure from Egypt. (Deuteronomy
> 16:3)

As people of the Christ event, we must understand

that a good relationship requires more than words of praise being spoken every so often. God performed the greatest of actions by giving his Son as a way for us to be able to be on intimate terms with him. So we worship him by not neglecting to keep that event and our resultant relationship in the forefront of our minds. This intentional living as people of the Christ event attributes worth to him.

I (David) have had to learn to purposely set aside my work in order to give Karen the attention she deserves as my wife. That lets her know she's worth a lot to me. Our spouses are often good at letting us know when our priorities are out of sequence! But sometimes it's a little harder with the Lord. That's why we set up reminders throughout the day, week, and year to keep our focus on Christ—to keep him in his rightful place.

Seems like a tall order, doesn't it? But the truth is, for many people this might not be as difficult as it sounds. What are some ordinary things we can do to center our lives on the Lord?

We can make Sunday special. For the Hebrews, the weekly Sabbath was a time in which they would realign their lives with what was most important. For six days the men and women were workers, but the seventh day they became worshippers. The Sabbath, in contrast to the rest of the week, reminded people that Jehovah was special and that it was imperative to remain in proper relationship with him. This re-centering their lives upon the Lord was all a part of worshipping him.

A corresponding way we Christians attribute

worth to God, or allow him to be central to how we live, is by making Sunday the high point of our week. We know Christ isn't more present or less present on Sunday than he is on Monday, Tuesday, . . . etc. But in a sense Sunday isn't like any of those other days. Why is that? Because through the years the church has declared Sunday to be the day we corporately worship the Lord. This is our weekly Sabbath when, like the Jews, we refocus our life-vision and make sure God remains in his rightful place in our lives.

For the Orthodox Jew, Sabbath is so important it takes three days to get ready for it, then three days to reflect on the wonder of what transpired. With this kind of thinking, there's a gentle rhythm to the week—three days moving upward toward the pinnacle, Sabbath, then three days to come down off the spiritual high.

Maybe you've noticed that most people have a high point to their week. For some it's payday, when they can go shopping, or take in a night of dinner and movies with friends, or go out on a date with someone special. For some a family gathering, a trip to the symphony, or an evening class is the emphasis of the week. Most people live looking forward to something, even if it's nothing more than a night to go to Blockbuster Video and get some film they've always wanted to see.

For other folks a sporting event is the highlight of the week. Consider a football fan who lives for the Sunday afternoon game. On Thursday he's thinking about the injuries on both sides—who will be able to play, and who won't? On Friday he looks at the odds on the teams and reasons through his opinion on which one is going to win. Saturday he's reviewing the picks of the experts and listening to the sports talk shows. The thing that grabs his attention on Sunday is not the pastor's sermon, but the time: Will he get out of church early enough to watch the opening kick-off? Once the game starts, it takes precedence over the phone, the family, and the jobs around the house.

Even when it's all over, the football enthusiast's mind hasn't stopped digesting what happened. He begins reliving the key plays—watching the evening news until the sportscast is on, and reading the newspaper first thing the next morning. Tuesday he's analyzing what the victory or loss means. Wednesday holds the last savoring of crucial moments while putting the past week's wins and losses into perspective: Does his team have a chance at the Superbowl? Before you know it, Thursday has come, and the process starts all over.

Now, there's nothing wrong with football ... or music ... or food ... or business ... or movies ... or other things you anticipate—until they become the focal point of your life. The Lord jealously desires that place for himself, and considering what he has done for us, he deserves it. So looking forward to the highlight of the week is fine; we just need to be sure that spotlight is on the right event.

It's a great privilege to have been raised in a church family, as both Laurie and I were. People with this background have learned to make church attendance a good habit. Our challenge is to get you to push past the established routine and to make your observance of the Lord's day an authentic worship experience.

You can do so by honestly saying to the Lord, "The reason I'm in your house each Sunday is because you are central to how I live. Going to church is not just a custom. I'm going because the greatest event that ever happened—the birth, life, death, and resurrection of your Son—is what has shaped my life. Father God, even if my mouth isn't as filled with praises as I would like, be aware that my actions declare where my heart is—always revolving around you!"

We can mark the yearly high points. The same kind of emphasis can be given to the church calendar. God has not established annual feasts for the church the way he did for the tribes of Israel. But certain times, such as the birth, death, and resurrection of our Lord, seem obvious days for Christians to observe.

If you were God and you gave your only Son to die for the people you loved, wouldn't you think it strange if the only comment someone made on Good Friday was, "Thank God it's Friday"? When we don't take time to think about the crucifixion on Good Friday, or we grouchily slump in to church on Easter Sunday because we stayed up to watch a late movie, we stand a good chance of offending God.

Do you know anyone who doesn't celebrate Christmas? It's nearly impossible to ignore this holiday in a culture that starts flaunting Santa Clauses and colored lights in early November. But with the way most of America observes Christmas, we may easily forget the "reason for the season." It would be ridiculous to give gifts at a birthday party to everyone except the one who was born on that day. In the same way, we need to make sure Christmas is a time when Christ is honored above all. His coming must be in the center of our minds throughout the holiday time.

Do you feel hurt when people forget to buy you a gift, send you a card, or call you on significant days? The church calendar has been set up to remind us of occasions that are important to God. Those are the times we need to be notably considerate of his feelings—his joy on Christmas, his sorrow on Good Friday, and his triumph on Easter.

From Advent all the way through Ascension Sunday and Pentecost, Christians can revolve their year around the Christ event. Church services might reflect pertinent themes through sermons, songs, banners, or responsive readings. Parents may read or tell their children stories that present what happened in Christ's life during each season of the year. We can even wear certain colors or put specific decorations up in our houses to constantly keep before us the meanings behind each stage of the year.

But always, our worship involves rotating each year around the Christ event. That's one basic way we acknowledge our King as the center of our lives. And attributing worth to him this way establishes

God in his rightful place.

We can meet daily with the Lord. We have briefly looked at making Sunday special and marking the yearly high points. Now let's figure out a way to make Christ central to more than the year or the week—by meeting with him daily.

I (Laurie) used to think of daily devotions as a discipline I endured for my own good. I felt I needed to spend time in Scripture and pray each day if I wanted to mature in my Christian walk. That's true, but now I'm viewing my time with God in a new way. It's a practice of showing Christ that I truly want to make him the center of my life. Like the weekly Sabbath cycle, I look forward to this quiet time in my day, and I reflect back upon it when it's over.

This is only one of many ways I am choosing to attribute worth to God. But it's an important one. When I set priority time aside to talk with him and to study what he did for me, I'm letting him know he's not in an I'll-get-with-you-if-I-can-fit-it-in category. Rather, Christ is the pivotal point around which my life functions. I never want to forget I'm a person of the Christ event, so I remind myself each day by spending time talking with my Lord and reflecting upon the greatest thing that ever happened—Christ's coming to earth so I could be one of God's children.

A daily Bible story time can be a good way to help children keep the Christ event in the forefront of their minds. When I was young, my parents bought a twelve-volume set of Bible stories. Each chapter had a beautiful illustration of that passage, and the words were simple and up-to-date, so I could easily understand them. My father would read one story to the family at breakfast each day, but because I was old enough to read them by myself, I would sneak the books off their shelf and read ahead. (I hate to say how often I did this when I was supposed to be dusting the living-room furniture!)

When I read the stories about Jesus, I would envision myself in the setting–sitting on Christ's lap with the rest of the children, gaping with the disciples as he walked on water toward us, or falling at the Lord's feet with Mary Magdalene on Resurrection morning. I didn't understand back then that I was worshipping God by filling my mind with the Christ event, but now I see how easy and important it can be to let stories teach children the significance of who Jesus is and what he has done for us.

New Ways to Integrate the Event into Our Lives

Let's explore some other elementary ways to keep before us this most important truth, that the living, dying, and rising of Christ is the greatest thing that has ever happened. What's more, we can examine how this great event continues in our own time. Christ has not finished working in the world, and paying close attention to how he's active in and through his people is another way we center our lives on him. We lend credence to our words of praise by regularly reminding ourselves of what

Christ did for us, and also by recognizing what he continues to do in our behalf.

Certain common practices at church, at home, and in "the world" (anywhere outside our usual religious setting) can remind us of what Jesus did and continues to do for us. These activities help us keep the Lord at the core of our lives.

We can be people of the event at home. My (David's) wife, Karen, has a collection of angels with which she has decorated our home. Each one is sculpted in stone, carved in wood, molded in brass, or cast in porcelain, and they're all beautiful. But they are also her way of saying, "Lord, just as the angels announced your coming to earth, so I want them to constantly proclaim in our home that you came to earth, lived, died, and rose again." Maybe you have religious art hanging on your walls, or a coffee table book containing artistic paintings of Jesus. This surrounding of ourselves with reminders of the birth, life, death, resurrection, and ascension of the Lord attributes worth to him by allowing the story of the Christ event to remain alive and well in our surroundings.

Journaling is becoming increasingly popular among Christians. It's amazing how many people do this each day. Recording what the Lord does in a notebook, or a blank-paged paperback, or even a computer file, helps us keep in mind that our lives revolve around the God who not only did a great thing in the past, but who continues to work today. The 50-Day Spiritual Adventure, in which over half a million people across the country participate each year prior to Easter, is one journaling program that many have found effective. In any case, if you're just beginning with this discipline, don't get discouraged. Give yourself time to learn how to journal. You'll soon be adept at putting down on paper the way Christ interacts with you each day.

Recently I (David) got a phone call from a friend from Portland. Gwen has been working for several years on a theatrical version of Karen's and my book, *Tales of the Resistance*. She nearly shouted in joy across the miles because *Tales* had been accepted for production by a theater in Seattle. The telephone is another way Christian friends can share with one another the great things Christ continues to do. Communication should go far beyond surface things. Christians can talk with one another in town or across many miles about what they're learning about the Christ event and how God is working in their lives.

Music is an obvious way to keep in mind the Christ event. Maybe you know an elderly person who softly hums the old hymns about Christ as she goes through her day:

> Tell me the story of Jesus,
> Write on my heart every word;
> Tell me the story most precious,
> Sweetest that ever was heard.
>
> Tell of the cross where they nailed him,
> Writhing in anguish and pain;
> Tell of the grave where they laid him,
> Tell how he liveth again.

Perhaps you find yourself singing "The Old Rugged Cross" or "Christ the Lord Is Risen Today" as you're cleaning up the dinner dishes. Or one way you relax is to listen to Handel's *Messiah* or Bach's *St. Matthew Passion.* Contemporary Christian music is prominent these days—you may hear it around the house or on your way to work. As you listen, try to picture what's happening in the song. Allow Jesus to touch you through the words. You'll be surprised at how your life can be influenced by reliving the Christ event through the imagination God has given you. Each song that tells the story of Jesus, each piece that suggests to us what Christ did in our behalf, is another way for us to think about the greatest event in history. It's also a constant reminder to us of our King's rightful place in our lives.

We can be people of the event at church. You may or may not sing hymns around your home, but more likely than not, you do sing them in church. Singing the hymns about our Lord is a way of corporately telling each other what he's done for us. That's encouraging, both to God and to us!

You probably see or hear the story of the Christ event in other ways in the sanctuary. Symbols in the church retell what Christ has done for us. The cross is in this category: it stands at the head of many churches as the ultimate symbol of our Lord's great sacrifice. Churches display banners portraying Christ's glory. Stained-glass windows show Jesus during different stages of his life—in the Garden of Gethsemane, for instance, or on the Mount of

Transfiguration. And believe it or not, even the "gift thermometer"—which records how financially close a church is to its goal of building a new sanctuary, starting an elementary school, or simply meeting its budget—can be a way to trace God's work in our church today! That's a reminder of how Christ continues to do great things for us.

The sermon, in many respects, is a retelling of the story of Christ. The preacher's job is to help us understand the Christ event, which happened so long ago and has progressed by the movement of the Holy Spirit down through the ages. What's more, the lesson teaches us how God's past and present work affects our lives. So a pastor, no matter how routine it may seem, should never tire of preparing a sermon. And we, no matter how tempted, should never allow ourselves to daydream while it's being delivered (ouch, that hurts)! The sermon should help us to be people of the event—it gives us material to meditate upon during the week, and it applies (or *should* apply) to our everyday lives the significance of what Christ did for us.

Church ought to provide many opportunities for us to tell what Christ is doing in our behalf. I (Laurie) remember having "testimony services" on Sunday nights when I was young. On occasion, these were lively—in fact, if you look at revival history, some of the greatest movements of the Spirit were carried forth by testimonies more than by preaching! By the time I reached my teens, however, the idea seemed to have become antiquated. When my pastor-father would announce a testimony service, I could hear a few groans (usually from the "teenager rows," but I did catch a sigh or two from the adults). Maybe that's because church testimonies are too often stale—just people rehashing things that happened years ago. Testimony services need to stay current as well as vibrant. We need to be eager to announce, "This is what the Lord is doing today!"

If we're lacking in dynamic testimony services in the church, we can at least be encouraged that many congregations are shifting toward developing small groups. In these house-groups, people study what Christ has done and share what he is doing in their lives on a more intimate basis. Small group meetings allow uninhibited disclosure of the continuation of the Christ event because they are usually free from distractions, and the people in the group feel comfortable with and enjoy each other. That's splendid, because when we let our social time revolve around the Lord, we put him in his rightful place—the center of our lives.

We didn't mention the Lord's Table in this section, even though it does apply to reliving the Christ event in church. We're saving Communion for the next chapter, so stay tuned!

We can be people of the event in the world. I (Laurie) grew up in a church that put a huge emphasis on missions. The sermons I remember most were the ones missionaries delivered—I was always intrigued with their stories of eating worms because that was what their host served them! I also remember the sense I would get of what great power the story of Jesus had on people who had never heard it. That's something I don't ever want to forget. If you are able to contribute through your church toward telling the story of the Christ event to those in other countries, do so! But even if that's not possible, we all have the chance to share the Christ event with people in the world right outside our front door.

When we invite others to attend church with us, or when we share with them what God is presently doing for us, our words express, "Jesus is extremely important to me, and I'm anxious that you meet him. I want to share this part of my life with you because if you don't know anything about it, you won't really know anything about me." We make an announcement to the world: "God's place is number one in my life." And as you know, this is worship.

These things can all contribute to regularly reminding ourselves of what Christ has done and continues to do. The miracle of his life, death, and resurrection—and the wonders he grants us each day—must never become "ho-hum."

We don't want to be like the people in the Ephesian church whom Jesus admonished in Revelation 2. He said, "I know your deeds, your hard work and your perseverance.... Yet I hold this against you: You have forsaken your first love." They had the Christian lifestyle down pat, but their attitude was wrong. They had stopped reminding themselves how thrilled they were when first forgiven, or how they wanted so much to master the Scriptures, or how they avidly shared with their friends what God was doing. We need to allow this early love to distinguish us as people of the Christ event. Never forgetting this love keeps our lives centered on the One who so deserves it.

I (Laurie) confess I had trouble grasping this chapter's concept when David first introduced it to me. It can be tough, because most of the things we've mentioned have been integral to my lifestyle for many years. I'd never thought of them as worship. They were too familiar, too easy.

Finally, during one of our writing meetings, the proverbial light bulb over my head blinked on. "Do you mean," I asked, "that all these things I've been doing as long as I remember—Bible story reading, going to church, singing songs, all those things that are a normal part of my life—are actually *worship*?"

And David, smiling because I'd finally caught on, said, "Yes! You're attributing worth to God by letting what he did and what he is doing touch every corner of your life. You don't usually notice you're doing this because you learned as a child to revolve your whole life around Jesus. But remember, when you're intentional about what you're doing, then you're putting God in his rightful place. And that, of course, is a way to attribute worth to him."

You see, being people of the event really isn't as hard as it sounds. If next Christmas you were to get a phone call that said you'd won the Discover

Card sweepstakes, you'd easily spend lots of time contemplating and retelling that moment when you first realized what was happening. And you would change your lifestyle because you'd suddenly have more money than you needed—that would just be a typical way the event would shape your life.

How much more passionate we should be about always holding in our minds the Christ event. The Son of God actually became a man, lived, died, and rose again on this small planet all because he loves us. And he continues to work each day in our behalf. How amazing! Why *wouldn't* we center our lives on him? The fact is, worshipping as people of the event is our natural response to the greatest thing that ever happened.

For Discussion and Reflection

1. Tell about a time you forgot what someone else considered an important event in his or her life.

2. How does remembering or not remembering certain events indicate our feelings toward the people involved in those experiences? How does this answer relate to your attitude toward God?

3. Explain why the Lord would find it important that the Christ event be at the very core of our lives.

4. What would have to happen in your life for church on Sunday to be the high point of your week?

5. Do you feel paying more attention to the church calendar would help you focus more on Christ? Why or why not?

6. Explain how some of the things Christians do every day, every week, or every year can actually be worship. What do you need to do to keep this understanding in mind?

Readings

I grew up in a home where the Old Testament was honored and Jews were lovingly regarded. For this reason, I remember Jewish friends clear back into my childhood. But I recall the different relationship I sensed the first time I attended a synagogue service. There, in the midst of a Hebrew congregation, I found that I had entered the historical Hebrew tradition that reached clear back to the days before Christ. I sensed I was not only participating in an event, but in an actual history, in a culture brought into existence by God and preserved for centuries in spite of setbacks, losses, and holocaust.

I discovered through my experience in the synagogue that the worship of Israel is rooted in the Exodus-event. I experienced how, through the retelling and the drama of the Exodus-event, Israel continually actualizes its own existence as the people of God. In that worship, my Jewish friends became once again the people of the Exodus-event....

Hebrew worship recalls the Exodus-event and looks forward to the Promised Land. As this true story is rehearsed again and again in various ways, God is praised for his faithfulness. Remembering the faithfulness of God, the people are to live out this story, allowing its hope to shape their personal and corporate lives....

Like Hebrew worship, primitive Christian worship was very event-oriented. This connection to Hebrew worship is only now being rediscovered by current biblical and liturgical scholars. So there remains a great deal of confusion about the most fundamental question worshiping churches must address: What is Christian worship? . . .

The heavenly picture of worship is clear: Worship represents Jesus Christ through re-presentation. Worship tells and acts out the living, dying, and rising of Christ. Worship celebrates Christ's victory over evil, the certain doom of Satan, and the promise of a new heaven and a new earth. A brief yet comprehensive definition of worship is worship celebrates God's saving deed in Jesus Christ. This kind of worship is not a goal-driven worship, but a Christ-driven worship. And when Christ is the center of worship, all of the goals for worship are achieved: Christ-centered worship educates, evangelizes, heals, develops spirituality—and is most enjoyable.

A Christ-centered worship—which is event-oriented worship—can never be static and merely intellectual because what happens is an actual and real communication of the power and benefit of the life, death, and resurrection of Christ. Worshiping churches recognize that every gathering of worship is ultimately a praise and thanksgiving for the overthrow of evil by God in Christ. This victory not only happened two thousand years ago, but it happens today in the lives of people who bring to worship their own struggles against that evil which shatters relationships, oppresses the poor, and brings constant dislocation into life.

The event of Christ is the only event in human history that promises relocation and centering, meaning and purpose. The promise and its fulfillment evoke passionate and heartfelt praise and thanks, especially for those aware of their own brokenness and the healing which Christ brings into their lives. For this reason, worshiping churches are returning to the biblical focus of worship—a celebration of the work of Christ characterized by a spiritual immediacy that touches people where they are. In this kind of worship, God breaks in and becomes present to touch our lives and create us anew.

(Robert Webber, *Signs of Wonder* [Nashville: Star Song, 1992], pp. 31–34)

●●●●●●●

As we think about worship, in Scripture and in the church's history, we can begin to discern three levels of worship. If the early Christians, for instance, distinguished themselves by being worshipers of Christ, what did this look like? What was involved?

(1) *Personal devotion to Jesus.* The ancient Roman might have prayed to Fortuna for good luck. The Christian communicated with God through Christ. And that still sets us apart. The Muslim prays to Allah, the Buddhist meditates on the teachings of Buddha, the Mammon-worshiper counts his money. But the Christian interacts on this personal level with Christ.

(2) *Obedience.* Christians became known in the Roman Empire for their lifestyles of love and morality. They obeyed Christ's teachings. This was what attracted people to Christianity in spite of the flare-ups of persecution. The Roman religions were gen-

erally devoid of moral teaching. The Romans did, however, require obedience to the laws of Rome and ordered residents of the empire to show their loyalty by worshiping the spirit of Caesar. This the Christ-worshipers refused to do.

Today worshipers of all kings show their loyalties in their daily lives. The Buddhist not only meditates on Buddha's words but applies them to his life. The Muslim tries to win the world for Allah. The modern Fortuna-worshiper plays the lottery every morning. The money-lover compounds his investments.

The Christian worships Jesus by obeying him in showing love to others and in matters of personal holiness.

(3) *Corporate commitment.* Devotees of the various religions of Rome would meet regularly with their groups to honor their gods. There were banquets, orgies, sacrifices, and other rituals. Many of these groups had elaborate temples where they held their meetings.

The Christians also met regularly together, usually in houses. They also shared meals, prayed together, sang together, and were instructed in the faith. Often under threat of arrest and death they met, but they met. That was an integral part of what it meant to be a Christian, to be a part of the Christian church, to meet for worship with other Christians.

And so today, even in an age of isolation, we see various temples in our cities. Less formal "worship" may go on at ballgames and rock concerts.

But Christians still worship Christ by joining with other Christians. Thus we signal our allegiance.

(Randy Petersen, *Giving to the Giver: Worship that Pleases God* [Wheaton, Ill.: Tyndale House, 1990], pp. 5-6)

••••••

Three annual pilgrim festivals shaped Hebrew life and gave it a distinctly spiritual cast: the Passover (April), the Feast of Weeks (late May/early June), and the Feast of Tabernacles (October). The festivals of our North American culture—both those with Christian origins and the secular ones—give shape to our lives too, and we have come to observe many of them in our churches. Often we don't even know why we observe one and not another. As Christians we should think about the festivals we observe and make conscious decisions about which ones are important for our church.

Several issues are involved. There is first of all the issue of how to handle secular holidays. Do we want to incorporate elements of the secular calendar like Memorial Day and Mother's Day, or do we want to keep only Christian holidays?

The answer to that question may be affected by the kind of church we are trying to be. For example, churches that see their Sunday morning services as a part of their evangelistic outreach often like to emphasize cultural holidays as a way of relating to the unchurched. Others, involved in "side door" rather than "front door" evangelism, limit special holiday emphases to that continuity can be given to systematic teaching of the Word from the pulpit. Missionary-minded churches elevate the importance of their missions conference. In the church in which I was reared, the greatest emphasis in the entire year was given to the missionary conference.

Bear in mind that you can have only a few prominent emphases in a church. You will be tempted to try to celebrate everything. Select the holidays and special observances that fit best with the church's vision for ministry.

During the Middle Ages the church calendar year became clogged with such a multitude of saint's days that the festivals capable of carrying the greatest theological weight—Christmas, Easter, Pentecost—were lost in the maze. Some of the Reformers reacted to this by dropping everything. John Calvin, for example, eliminated the entire church year. Other Protestants followed suit, and in the sixteenth century the Puritans rejected even Christmas as a festival day. As a result, evangelical churches today in the main tend to observe liturgical festival days with a minimum of pageantry.

In fact, in our time secular holidays like Independence Day and Mother's Day generally receive more emphasis in our churches than festival days like Pentecost, a day with momentous theological significance. If I could encourage you to think about just one festival, however, this would be the one. The coming of the Holy Spirit must rank as the single most important historic event in the New Testament subsequent to Jesus' ascension (another neglected holiday).

It is possible to opt for a simplified church year that reinforces the events that really matter—the birth, death, and resurrection of Jesus, and the giving of the Holy Spirit—without becoming encumbered by a host of unessential occasions. A simplified liturgical year, an unfamiliar though valuable concept, deserves a second look by Evangelicals.

(Barry Leisch, *People in the Presence of God: Models and Directions for Worship* [Grand Rapids: Zondervan, 1988], pp. 222–223)

••••••

to know him risen

Is it obliquely
  through time's telescope, thick-
  lensed with two thousand Easters?
Or to my ear in latin, three chanted
  'Kyries' triumphing over a purple chancel?
Or in a rectangular glance at sepia
  snap shots of Jerusalem's Historic Sites?
Can I touch him through the cliché crust
  of lilies, stained glass, sunrise services?
Is a symbol soluble?
Can I flush out my eyes and rinse away
  the scales?
Must I be there?
Must I feel this freshness
  at an interval of inches? and sense,
  incredulous, the reassurance of warm
  breath?
  and hear again the grit of stone
  under his sandal sole?
  those familiar Judean vowels

in the deep voicing of beatitude? recognize
the straight stance, quick eye,
strength, purpose, movement, clear
command—all the swift three-day antonyms
of death that spring up to dispel its sting,
to contradict its loss?
Must I be Thomas—belligerent in doubt,
hesitant, tentative, convinced, humbled,
loved, and *there*?
Must sight sustain belief?
Or is a closer blessedness
to know him risen—now
in this moment's finger-thrust of faith—here
as an inner eyelid lifts?

(Luci Shaw, *Polishing the Petoskey Stone*
[Wheaton, Ill.: Harold Shaw, 1990], p. 92.
Used by permission.)

●●●●●●

Come and see what God has done,
how awesome his works in man's behalf!
He turned the sea into dry land,
they passed through the river on foot—
come, let us rejoice in him.
He rules forever by his power,
his eyes watch the nation—
let not the rebellious rise up against him.

Praise our God, O peoples,
let the sound of his praise be heard;
he has preserved our lives
and kept our feet from slipping. . . .

Come and listen, all you who fear God;
let me tell you what he has done for me.

I cried out to him with my mouth;
  his praise was on my tongue.
If I had cherished sin in my heart,
  the Lord would not have listened;
  but God has surely listened
  and heard my voice in prayer.
Praise be to God,
  who has not rejected my prayer
  or withheld his love from me!
  (from Psalm 66)

Gathered 'Round the One Who Makes Things Better

People of celebration attribute worth to God by taking great delight in the presence of his Son.

Old Aunt Annie Vernarsdale was not much to look at, but she made delicious salmon patties. When I (David) was a boy during World War II, there was a shortage of pastors in the area. My father, a lay person, often drove to speak at a church ten miles away in tiny Maywood, Missouri. Given the choice, I would go with Dad. It was great being around him, and he told interesting stories in his sermons. Also, Aunt Annie habitually brought her fried salmon patties to the potluck that followed the service.

Toward the end of Dad's sermon, I could begin to taste that salmon in my mouth. I'd rub my pants and think, "Oh man, Dad, hurry up. I've got to get in line fast enough so I get one of those patties before everyone else beats me to them!"

I have always been a sucker for church potlucks. When people ask me, "Where's the best place in town to eat?" I reply, "If you're coming on a Sunday, the best place to eat is at church when they have a potluck. It doesn't cost you a dime, and they have the best food you'll find! Besides, no restaurant in town has a better atmosphere."

Celebrating His Presence

Do you know why the church's atmosphere is better than any other place? Because Jesus is there when we, his body, gather. He's there in our church services. But he's also in gatherings like potluck suppers after the service. What's more, he's there when we meet with other church folks in our homes. And whenever Jesus is recognized in his people's lives, we believe they enjoy themselves more than at any other time.

If you merely watched movies about Jesus, you might disagree with us. Usually Christ is portrayed as kind of a dour person. He says serious things all the time, and frankly, he's a little uninteresting. Don't you think that kind of portrayal is a bit one-dimensional? It's the opposite of the way we feel Jesus is. We're convinced he's full of life and likes entering into all different situations to make them better.

Remember the John chapter 2 story of Jesus at the Cana wedding? The poor host ran out of wine to serve his guests during the many hours of feasting. Jesus changed some ordinary water into wine and had servants take it to the banquet master, who exclaimed, "Hey! This is better than the wine we served before!" That's characteristic of the Jesus touch. Our Lord makes everything better—it becomes like wine of a vintage year! And knowing we're in the presence of the One who makes things better is good cause for us to celebrate.

You may be wondering, "Is every church potluck really supposed to be a celebration?" We would say yes: each time of fellowship should be a celebration of Christ's presence.

Now, before you start scratching your head and puzzling over this, let's figure out what it means to celebrate. The *American Heritage Dictionary* defines celebration as a time when we observe a day or event with ceremonies of respect, festivity, and rejoicing. If you look at this, you'll see there are two main aspects of celebration.

First, celebration respectfully *observes* a day or event. It sets apart a time as special. This is done with ceremony, which denotes a kind of formality. For instance, if you went to a birthday party, you would be commemorating a person's birth. It would be virtually impossible to have a birthday celebration without having someone special you're honoring. You set that time aside to gather with friends and relatives. There's a certain formality or ritual that goes along with birthday parties. You might tell stories of things your friend did when she was little, or commend her for the things she's accomplished through the years. Of course, you'd have a birthday cake, the blowing out of candles, plus gift opening. When you look closely at all of this, you find an earnest, reflective side of you that wishes your friend well and hopes she has many pleasant years ahead of her.

Secondly, celebration *rejoices* in festivity. This part is just plain old fun; it's a time of kicking back and enjoying each other and the person or occasion you're remembering. What would a birthday party be without games or laughter? In fact, you wouldn't call it a celebration if you didn't think you'd enjoy anything about the occasion. That just wouldn't make sense.

Any major celebration you think of has these two elements—respectful observation, remembrance, or at least a repeated "ritual" that sets the time apart as special, and naturally, a time of festivity or rejoicing. We celebrate the Fourth of July by remembering the signing of the Declaration of Independence—and by gazing at fireworks and having picnics. We celebrate Bonnie Blair's winning her fifth Olympic speed skating gold medal by watching (in person or via television) her award ceremony and commending all her skill and hard work—and by cheering like mad, or in Bonnie's own words, "crying, screaming, yelling, and laughing all at once" because we're so happy for her.

We do *not* celebrate Good Friday; we observe, or commemorate it, but we lose that second joyful aspect that makes the day a true celebration. We do celebrate Easter, however; we remember that Christ rose from the grave—and we dress up in bright colors, sing exuberant songs, eat a big meal with family, and generally rejoice that Jesus is alive!

That's the way it is when we celebrate Christ's presence. We keep in mind who he is and what he means to us (we covered some of that when we wrote about being people of the event). And we laugh and have a good time together because we enjoy being with Christ and with his body, the church.

Celebration attributes worth to God. Let's relate this to worship. Suppose someone wealthy and generous gave one of us a free trip to Acapulco. Either David or Laurie would be flown down first-class and put up in the finest hotel. All expenses would be paid, and part of the trip would include seeing the cliff-divers who risk their lives jumping into the sea. A Mexican fiesta would be on the agenda, and there'd be a generous supply of pesos to spend at "el mercado."

"What about Karen?" David would ask. "Is she included in your invitation?" Laurie would want to know the same thing about Joel. Why? Because when you're still in love after thirty-two years of marriage, or even after just one year, nothing seems as pleasant if your mate isn't with you. Karen's the person I (David) love to be around more than anyone else. And when I (Laurie) go anyplace exciting, I can't even imagine having a good time without my best friend Joel.

What we're emphasizing is that we delight in the presence of our spouses. That's one way we attribute worth to them. Our attitudes of celebrating their presence make them feel appreciated and let them know they're very important to us.

In a similar fashion, when we delight in being where Jesus is we attribute worth to him. On the negative side, when someone doesn't like you, or appears to be avoiding you, how do you react? You sense that something is wrong with you—it makes you feel humiliated or angry. But when someone says the simple five-word sentence, "I really enjoy your company," it makes your day!

Taking great pleasure in Christ's presence is one

of the ways we worship him. Choosing to get involved in church gatherings is a way of honoring our Lord. "Jesus," we say, "we praise you with our words and by centering our lives on who you are and what you did, but also by participating in activities we can enjoy together. Thank you for letting us rejoice in your presence!"

Celebration was present in the early church. Sometimes in the modern church we get more serious about the Lord than we should. That's not to say we should take him *lightly*; rather, we should take him with *delight.* The New Testament house churches enjoyed more of a flavor of food and fellowship and comradery than we realize. When meeting in homes with approximately twenty or thirty people, it's hard to imagine being greeted at the door and handed a church bulletin!

Picture instead the exchange of spiritual experiences that must have been common in these gatherings. Let your ears "hear" the laughter as people related how Christ was working despite the difficulties in their culture. Allow your nose to pick up some of the smells of cheeses, breads, and fruits. Feel the mingling of the earthy bodies; catch the jubilant mood. Do you suppose the people are having a good time, or are they there because they feel obliged to attend? That's one way to perceive whether Christ is present.

We're sure God wanted his first followers to enjoy themselves. And why would he desire anything different for us today? In the Old Testament we read the following words, and we can take their overarching attitude to heart:

> Celebrate (that's right, celebrate) the Feast of
> Tabernacles for seven days after you have
> gathered the produce of your threshing floor
> and your winepress. Be joyful at your Feast—you,
> your sons and daughters, your menservants and
> maidservants, and the Levites (the religious lead-
> ers), the aliens, the fatherless and the widows
> who live in your towns (sounds like *everybody*,
> doesn't it?). For seven days celebrate (understand,
> this is *seven days* of celebration!) the Feast to the
> LORD your God at the place the LORD will choose.
> For the LORD your God will bless you in all your
> harvest and in all the work of your hands, and
> your joy will be complete (What will be complete?
> Just wanted to make sure you didn't miss it).
>
> Deuteronomy 16:13-15 [parenthetical comments
> ours]

Celebration is prevalent in African-American services. Before taking up broadcasting, I (David) spent twelve years in inner-city ministry. I came to the conclusion while working there that the African-American church is much better at celebrating than the white church is. My black friends came to church prepared to have a good time. They entered into the worship whole-heartedly. Church was often a five- or six-hour experience, including food and fellowship. There was none of the "arrive right on time, expect to leave in exactly an hour, pass a little small-talk in the vestibule, and be on my way" attitude I see today! Maybe we need a willingness to "waste" our time in church in order to truly celebrate being with Christ and his people.

Celebration pervades a healthy church. One of the traits of a dysfunctional family is its inability to celebrate. We fear it's one of the traits of a dysfunctional church family as well. Yes, there's a danger of having too good a time. Church people can gather in Christ's name and entirely forget that the Lord is present. A congregation can get so self-focused it forgets its mission to outsiders. But we can also dishonor God by losing our joy, which leaves us with truncated worship—all lofty words, but no delight factor; all head, but no heart.

Have you ever been to a Sunday school picnic? Three-legged races and little tots playing "pick up the peanuts," mass quantities of food and picnic tables lined end to end can all be a part of celebrating Christ's presence. These activities commend the church and applaud the Lord—he is the center of our time together and the reason we enjoy each other's company. To make sure we don't forget about him, we sing choruses together with guitars and tambourines under a pavilion when the sun starts to go down.

One thing I (Laurie) remember feeling at those picnics was that our group was different from any others in the park. I have specific images in my head of a bunch of young people hanging out toward the entrance to the park, drinking and swearing. They were all wearing cutoff jeans (a "no-no" way back then among "decent" people), and I was astonished that they had so much skin showing!

I remember feeling unsafe around those people and very secure with my Sunday school group.

I was aware of the oneness of this family, a family that was bigger than my immediate five-person cell. I felt protected and loved; I understood the church people were good to be around. They were a peculiar people, to be sure, but at the same time I liked that peculiarity—it seemed to make everything better. And now I know why I felt that way: Jesus was there with us.

At the same time, at those church celebrations everyone seemed more human than angelic. And that was reassuring! Certain Sunday school teachers took on a whole different personality when we had a church picnic. They weren't nearly as authoritative; they didn't try to be super-spiritual. If they tripped on the park's uneven stone stairs, or they struck out when up to bat, they might even have said some terrible word, like "Drat!" Then I would end up thinking, "Oh, he's human after all! Good!" That's part of what makes a church get-together so healthy. We feel more footloose and fancy-free because Christ is there, and we are celebrating his presence.

We need to bring this comfortable celebration into the church family. When you're little you might not have the ability to point out a healthy situation, or "practice the presence of Christ," because that's just not terminology you understand. But as you look back over the years with perspective, you know when you felt like you belonged. You are aware that Jesus was with those church folks, and you have this vision of him enjoying his time with you, and of him laughing. That's just one illustration of a healthy church worshipping the Lord.

It's a win-win situation. God enjoys it when we enjoy him, and vice versa. Why would we ever hold back from this wonderful experience?

Learning to Delight in the Lord

Why, indeed, do we ever have trouble celebrating? I (David) sometimes think about Mrs. Lockenby, who taught Sunday school and seemed extremely rigid. I thought she had pure ice water in her veins, because if anyone in the class wiggled even just a little while she was doing her flannelgraph lesson, he (or she, but usually it was a he) had to stand in the corner for what seemed like the longest time. I wonder now whether Mrs. Lockenby was someone who enjoyed celebrating. Did she really delight in spending time with the little members of the body of Christ?

And what about those who seem nice enough, but never have the time, the money, or even the interest they need for celebrating? What about when they "just can't seem to get into it"? Are they somehow banned from this facet of worship, simply because that's not the way their lives are set up? Is celebration something that just happens, or is it something we need to cultivate?

I (David) believe it would please God if we did take time to learn how to delight in his presence. And one of the first steps that many people need to take is to determine to enjoy themselves. I have written before about my workaholism; it's something that's liable to get in the way of my delight in celebration. Lately I've resolved to come together with my own family and with the family of God, to leave behind my work and fully partake of the celebration at hand. I'm becoming better and better at it (Laurie agrees)! But it's a learning process.

We can begin delighting in celebration by readjusting our thinking. Sometimes church people can be sour. Have you noticed? It's not that they never find it within themselves to smile, but they consider the crazy things young people or certain other groups do as trivial or superfluous. *Why,* they wonder, *do we need a senior citizens' roller skating group, anyway?*

Our answer is simple: These church-based groups are an excuse to get together and celebrate with the people of God. What are we celebrating? We're remembering that Christ is in our midst when two or three gather in his name, and we're rejoicing, having a good time, because he is there!

Maybe you need to learn to accept the Middle-Aged-and-Marrieds Bowling League or the Relief-for-Moms-in-Summertime Craft Club. You needn't worry that your church will become a mere "social congregation" as long as a degree of intentionality is in the activity. People are there to celebrate their common life in Christ. They get together because they'd rather be with the people of God than with anyone else in the world. As long as that conviction is in the middle of all their laughter and revelry, Jesus is honored. That attributes worth to him.

You can begin to delight in celebration by sharing your memories of good times with God and with others. Whether they're telling them or listening to them, people get a kick out of stories. The funniest things happen when we're with God's people, especially when we think everything's supposed to be very celestial, but we end up seeing—or doing—something most improper!

Among the older members of the church I (Laurie) grew up in, legend has it that during the sixties, when it was fashionable to be hairy, Edith and Sam Micelli's son, Paul, sported a long hairdo. It was complete with a full moustache and beard. Paul was popular among his friends and all the church folks, so he had a lively, "hip," high-school graduation party. But to his great embarrassment, my three-year-old mind had recently learned that Christ is always present with church people. Paul walked into the room, and with my finger pointed straight at him and in my piercing little girl voice, I cried, "Mommy, THERE'S JESUS!" I don't think I'll ever live that one down. Even though it happened long ago, the story pops up when we get together with the Micellis and other long-time church friends.

That's all part of how we can cultivate a "celebration attitude." When we repeat memories of funny things that happened and pleasant times we had—even if we simply had them because we were with such a good bunch of church people—we begin to delight in celebration. We can tell other people the stories. We may recount them for God. But all the time we're saying, "I hold these in my memory because they're part of the events that have great meaning to me. And God, they're significant to me because you were there when they happened, and you are important to me." That's worship.

Another way we can foster delight in celebration is by giving credit where credit is due. Charlie Hademan didn't seem like a spiritual giant. He wasn't outspoken; he didn't make people laugh; he wasn't a wonderful event organizer or piano player or prayer leader. But in every celebration I (David) remember taking place in one church I attended, Charlie was somehow involved. He was the pancake flipper for the men's breakfasts. He popped the popcorn for the kids' socials. He actually stayed to clean up after the Harvest potlucks. And I can't help but think that when it came to celebrations, Charlie Hademan was a fantastic worshipper.

A lot of people contribute to celebrating Christ's presence, but they're hardly ever recognized. A big part of delighting in celebration has to do with appreciating and recognizing those people. Commending hard workers solidifies in everyone's mind that celebration is not all fun and games. It has a certain serious formality—all the work done in Christ's name—without which the big bash would never exist. And what's more, getting the credit due them can help those doing the work to delight all the more in remembering the reason for their labor.

You might go back to the kitchen during the next Youth Group Spaghetti Dinner to thank Mr. Donardia for making those fifty pounds of spaghetti. Or, after the Easter service, you could search for Mrs. Roust, who made such a lovely flower arrangement for the Communion table. Or, gratefully shake the hand of young Kathy the cellist, who sat in the balcony throughout the choir cantata, but added so much to the church atmosphere during intermission. Making sure that long-overdue credit is given, being certain you have the appropriate appreciation in your own heart, says to the Lord, "So many things contribute to a wonderful celebration. These people helped make your presence all the more obvious to me. I want to regularly say thank you to the faithful ones who help me rejoice in you."

You can learn to delight in the celebration of Christ's presence by committing yourself to being hospitable. There are few things that help a celebration along more than a spirit of hospitality. A hospitable attitude welcomes people in the name of Christ. It says to each person who enters the door, "Come in! The Lord is here, and we'd love to celebrate his presence with you."

Do you know that you don't need to be the host of the party to be hospitable? Remember the story of the sinful woman in Luke 7:36-50. The Pharisee with whom Jesus was eating had not shown much hospitality, but the woman who had washed her Lord's feet with tears, wiped them with her hair, and anointed his head with oil, made up for the host's lack. Jesus commended the woman for her faith and forgave her sins. But he must have appreciated her hospitality, because he reprimanded the Pharisee for not showing him the courtesy he deserved as the guest of the house. Hospitality says, "Every guest here deserves courtesy, and I am happy to be the one who shows it. I'll receive each person as I would receive Christ, because each one is a member of his body."

There are two angles to being hospitable, and we find them both in the story of Mary and Martha of Bethany. Martha was the eldest sister, and she invited Jesus to stay with them while he was in town. "She had a sister called Mary, who sat at the Lord's feet listening to what he said. But Martha was distracted by all the preparations that had to be made." When she complained to Jesus about the unfair situation, he said, "Martha, Martha . . . you are worried and upset about many things, but only one thing is needed. Mary has chosen what is better" (Luke 10:39-42).

It's okay to make a fuss when we have someone important staying with us. It's suitable to be sure that person is comfortable and well fed. That's one aspect of hospitality, and we suspect Jesus would classify it as good. But it's even more important to spend time with our guest, to enjoy his or her presence. In this situation, Jesus complimented Mary on choosing that side of hospitality. He classified her delight as something even better.

Behind her back, I (Laurie) call my mother-in-law "The Hospitality Queen" because she is more adept at blending these two aspects of hospitality than anyone else I know. Karen has taught me about doing things with a little bit of flair. Dressing up in a nice outfit, making an impressive centerpiece, setting the table just so, or providing little gifts for guests can communicate to them that they are important. But I've also learned from Karen's example that the *flair* must never take the place of the *fellowship*. If a special meal hasn't turned out quite right, it never seems to matter at the Mains house; the important thing is that the guests are there and everyone is able to enjoy each other's company. Karen's delight in celebrating their presence attributes worth to her guests. Her favorite way of balancing the special touches with taking pleasure in friends' company is by bringing them into the kitchen with her. They help make the meal, and she gets to talk and laugh with them. Too bad Martha didn't think of that—her preparations would have turned out much better if Jesus had been involved!

Celebration on Sunday

Whether or not we acknowledge it, celebration is built into our usual worship. In fact, when we think about worship, one day quickly jumps to mind—Sunday. Unfortunately, sometimes we don't comprehend that our worship services incorporate two actual celebrations.

Sunday is a day we have set aside to remember the Lord. Setting a day apart as special is one side of our definition of celebration. We often say we are *observing* the Lord's day. And we do this by going through a certain ritual: we don't just sleep in; instead, we dress up, get the whole household packed into the car, and drive to a building that's specifically built for this event. We might go to Sunday school to learn about and remember the Lord. We attend the worship service, which is usually a planned, or formal, ceremony in which similar things happen each week. This might all become rather tiresome for a man who has worked through the week and would rather spend his morning relaxing, or a mother who has to get four kids dressed and keep them all orderly until she can "set them loose" in Sunday school.

That's probably because the second side—the fun part—of the celebration is missing. Here, churches and families sometimes go awry. My (David's) wife Karen has written about this in her book, *Making Sunday Special*:

> I used to think this Sunday morning commotion ("Mo-om! Randy won't let me in the bathroom." BANG! BANG! "Hurry up! I gotta get in there!") was due to the fact that we were a ministerial family and some unbidden demonic force attempted to steal our good intents toward adoration. ("Who took my comb?" "Someone didn't put the milk back in the refrigerator last night!") . . . But then I discovered that many Christian families (not just those of us in pastoral ministry) had the same struggles. Sunday morning, leaving for church, was often the worst time in their week.
>
> As a couple, David and I vowed to work together to restore our observance of the Lord's Day, to seek to make Sunday the best day of the week, the high point. . . . We wanted Sunday to become the joyful focal point of our weekly lives. (pp. 19–20)

For most of us, making a unique, enjoyable occasion out of our Sunday worship ritual can be a new central theme. We can do this in our families by preparing ourselves on Saturday night (to avoid the

Sunday morning rush). We can also plan to spend select time together on Sunday as a family—we might prepare and eat a big meal together, go out to the park, or read a book as a group.

We can also do this within the church. Those weekly after-church potlucks sure made Sunday a celebration for me (David). We can try putting a little more joy into our song services; we could let the children do something out of the ordinary before the sermon; the introduction of art or drama or dance might give a service a better mood of celebration. And always, we must remember that Jesus is there in the center of our group. He's the one who makes everything better, and we can delight in allowing him to do that.

Communion is a celebration highlight of our church service. I (Laurie) will never forget the first time I took Communion. I was sitting about half-way back on the right-hand side of our oppressively silent church (we were charismatic, and it wasn't nearly that solemn at any other point in the service). I was about eight years old at the time—my father and mother wanted to be sure I was old enough to understand what I was doing so I wouldn't take it flippantly.

Well, a terrible thing happened. I got excited! My heart was pounding, and I felt like jumping up and singing, "I did it, I did it! Jesus is in me!" I was utterly ashamed of myself. How could I feel so happy when I was supposed to be remembering how Jesus died on the cross for my sins? Why should I want to dance and laugh when the rest of the people in the church were at their most prim and proper?

After that I partook of the Lord's Supper with conscientious sobriety.

Then, thirteen years later, I visited a liturgical worship service for the first time. Not realizing this church had the Eucharist every week, I was thrilled that I'd managed to come on their "Communion Sunday." The priest moved to the altar and led the people toward the Lord's Table: "On the night He was handed over to suffering and death, our Lord Jesus Christ took bread..."

But wait! He was smiling! And the deaconess who was helping him serve the elements had her head thrown back and her hands lifted up to heaven! The congregation was suitably quiet, but there was an unmistakable air of expectancy. And I felt again that excitement I'd known as an eight-year-old taking Christ's body and blood for the first time.

That was my introduction to celebrating the Lord's Supper in a new way. It went beyond the first stage of celebration—the respectful observation I'd always encountered in Communion services. It delved into the second aspect—the festive rejoicing indicated by the word *Eucharist,* or "great thanksgiving."

When we worship by celebrating the Lord's Supper, let's not forget to balance those two basics. It would be impossible to celebrate without reflecting upon the reason for the occasion. But it's just as impossible to celebrate without rejoicing. We should be completely exhilarated because the risen

Christ is right there with us at his Table.

Let's never lose the delight in celebrating Christ's presence. Our delight communicates to the Lord how important he is to our lives. That's worship to him, for it shows he's been put in the place he deserves.

When you're a child standing on tiptoe looking down that endless potluck table brim-full of Swedish meatballs, home-grown strawberries, and fudge brownies, church can be the best place on earth. Merriment, good memories, people you love, and looking forward to Aunt Annie Vernarsdale's fried salmon patties are all a part of being people of celebration. Nothing in the world could be better.

But that's primarily because Jesus is there. He's the One who makes everything better. And he takes pleasure in our enjoyment because he knows we're there to honor him. Try picturing the King at your next church fellowship. He'll be the one laughing with all the folks gathered around him. And he'll be saying, "Let the celebration begin!"

For Discussion and Reflection

1. What good memories do you have of church celebrations?

2. Tell about a Christian you know who is good at celebrating the presence of Christ.

3. How can you make Sunday worship a more joyous occasion in your home? In your church?

4. Is there something that consistently inhibits you from celebrating with the body of Christ? What is it?

5. The next time your church celebrates the Lord's Table, how can you make rejoicing a part of your participation?

6. What would you have liked about being a part of a New Testament house church?

Readings

The worship of the Christian church should be like a party for which God is host and to which everyone is invited. Worship is the celebration of the good news that man has a sponsor in the universe and a fellowship on earth. Jesus Christ said as much in the parable of the great feast (Luke 14:15-24; cf. Matt. 22:1-10), and the church at its best has understood Christ himself to be the life of the party.

Jesus likened life in the kingdom to a great feast. The image appeals to most of us because one of the most pleasant experiences of life is to attend a party thrown by a gracious host where we are among friends. We greet one another warmly, enjoy good food, talk over old times, share the good news and the bad, take a look at the future, and open ourselves to new possibilities. A distinctive element in this party in the parable is that an active invitation is extended to the outsider. The waiter is sent out to bring in people off the streets. Therein lies the embarrassment. . . . But the major point is clear: Jesus intends our fellowship with God and with one another to be a great celebration. This is the joyous revelation that lies at the heart of the current revolution in worship.

(David James Randolph, *God's Party: A Guide to New Forms of Worship* [Nashville: Abingdon Press, 1975], p. 17)

●●●●●●

On October 26 I witnessed the unrivaled joy of these people. It was Simhat Torah, the happiest of Jewish Holy Days, when the reading of the books of the law is completed for the year in the synagogue and Genesis is begun over again. I went to the Wailing Wall in the morning and found there the same throngs of black-clad Jews that I had seen before, bobbing and chanting in front of the stones, but here also were wildly shouting groups of men—well over a thousand of them—parading the huge parchment scrolls which had been brought forth from their synagogues. They put their hands on one another's shoulders and danced in a circle, shouting the praises of the Book, singing songs about the rebuilding of the Temple and the redemption of Jerusalem. Frequently I caught the words *Yerushalayim, Israel, simhat* (which I learned means "happy"), and *adonai,* the substitute for the ineffable name of God.

At the foot of the Wall, groups of men gathered with a prayer shawl held above them like a roof. This, I learned at last (for although the crowd was made up almost entirely of Jews, one after another told me he knew no more about what was happening than I did—I would have to ask a rabbi) was for the blessing of the scrolls. They would bring their scrolls—some were covered with large, elaborately filigreed silver cylinders, others with embroidered velvet sheaths, some topped by gold or silver crowns—and begin their own dance, weaving and circling among the others, eyes closed or lifted to heaven, bodies jerking and swaying with ecstasy, voices raised in lusty hymns. There were several oriental Jewish women sitting on a pile of rubble at one side, keening in the piercing, Arab ululation of joy or sorrow. When the men drew near with a scroll, these women rocked with ecstasy, throwing kisses toward the sacred book, with tears streaming down their dark cheeks. Now and then I caught the word *aleluyah* from their shrieks. The dancing men paused at intervals to embrace the scrolls, to kiss them and clasp them in their arms, lifting them high as a young and strong lover might do with the woman he loved, while the other men increased their shouts and some of them waved flags. There were children riding on the shoulders of their fathers, laughing with the excitement of it all, bouncing high and victorious above the crowd.

Not much emphasis was ever placed on plain human happiness in my religious training. Our gatherings were careful and quiet and controlled. The "joy of the Lord" was to us a deep, serious thing not connected with celebrating in any way, let alone with dancing, and to find myself confronted with this wild abandon and told that it was the celebration of the written Word gave me pause. Deuteronomy 12 speaks of the Jews living in the land which God gives them, destroying the places of worship belonging to strange deities and making sacrifices to the Lord God, "happy before the Lord in all your undertakings." Clearly the Jews had something here that the rest of us had missed.

(Elisabeth Elliot, *Furnace of the Lord: Reflections on the Redemption of the Holy City* [New York: Doubleday, 1969], pp. 89–90)

●●●●●●

I not only love to worship, I love to watch people

who are worshiping. The psalmist says, "It is fitting for the upright to praise him" (Ps. 33:1). I read that verse one day, and as I meditated on it, it struck me with its truth. Sometimes when I'm in a group of people who are worshiping, particularly if they are singing with their eyes closed and their hands raised, I'll take a peek at them. And I'm always impressed by how beautiful they look. People seem to glow and radiate when they worship.

I remember my grandmother used to say to me, "Oh Twila, blue is so becoming on you." She meant that I look good in blue. This idea also pertains to worship. Praise is becoming to the upright. When we worship, praise produces a radiant beauty on our faces because of our contact with God.

More important, in worship we are especially beautiful to God. Worship is a sweet aroma to God. For me, the fact that God loves our worship is a very challenging and motivating truth, a truth that I stress in all my worship songs. In my song, "This Celebration," I have tried to capture how our worship is pleasing to God. The song names who God is and praises God for God's person. Of course, this is what we do when we gather together to worship: we lift up our hearts in response to God.

> *Shout for joy unto the Lord of Hosts*
> *Celebrate His holiness, celebrate His power*
> *Shout for joy unto the Lord of Hosts*
> *Celebrate His mercy, celebrate His love*
> *Unto the King, this celebration*
> *Unto the King, Unto the King*
> *Unto the King, this celebration*
> *Unto the King, Unto the King*

(Twila Paris with Robert Webber, *In This Sanctuary: An Invitation to Worship the Savior* [Nashville: Star Song, 1993], pp. 21–22)

● ● ● ● ● ●

This Psalm [Psalm 95] says, "Venite!" "O come and shout to the Lord." These verbs in the first verse are verbs enjoining encouragement and mutual stimulation. The nature of these verbs may suggest that even people in Israel had to be encouraged to display their enthusiasm for God. They, as we, are instructed to "encourage one another" in public worship—"*and all the more as you see the Day approaching*" (Hebrews 10:25). . . .

> *Let us come before Him with public acknow-
> ledgement;*
> *let us shout joyfully to Him with melodies.*
> (our translation)

As we think about the application of this mood of worship to our own worship services, we find this mood has a special relevance in the areas of praise and music. This Psalm calls for exuberance and involvement, for joy and excitement as we adore our God and enjoy Him. . . .

Christianity Today ran a splendid article by J. Daniel Baumann on the importance of true worship. Baumann argued in that article that "biblical worship . . . is celebration"—the contention of our message. Baumann explains:

> That is not to say we are to be flippant or careless (see Psalm 89:7), nor that we gather in order to exchange emotional highs and get spiritual goose pimples. When I was a child, I was given to occasional restlessness during church services. I was

admonished to "sit still, you're in church." Somehow I got the wrong message. My folks never intended it—but I was getting the impression that God was a grouch; I wasn't convinced I could even enjoy him. I've chanced my mind, or, better yet, the Bible is changing my mind.

Baumann then insists that "the characteristic note of the Old Testament worship is exhilaration," and he encourages: "Let's have more spiritual celebration; the saints in Scripture did." Such is the mood of Psalm 95.

(Ronald Allen and Gordon Borror, *Worship: Rediscovering the Missing Jewel* [Portland, Oreg.: Multnomah Press, 1982], pp. 80–82)

●●●●●●

I said to the LORD, "You are my Lord;
    apart from you I have no good thing.
As for the saints who are in the land,
    they are the glorious ones in whom is
    all my delight. . . .
I will praise the LORD, who counsels me;
    even at night my heart instructs me.
I have set the LORD always before me.
Because he is at my right hand,
I will not be shaken.

Therefore my heart is glad and my tongue
    rejoices; my body also will rest secure . . .
You have made known to me the path of
    life; you will fill me with joy in your
    presence, with eternal pleasures at your
    right hand.
(from Psalm 16)

Going to the Extreme

People of service attribute worth to God as living sacrifices by ministering to others as they would to their King.

You're in a museum of ancient history, learning all you can about what was happening in the world between the years of the Old and the New Testament. A perky tour guide describes Alexander the Great and the rise of the Grecian empire.

She senses the group is getting restless, so in an attempt to keep everyone's interest, she stops in front of a picture of the great conqueror and tells the following story:

A young soldier serving under Alexander the Great ran in fright when his company was attacked. He didn't want to sacrifice his life, even though he had promised to serve his country and his commander.

That was a capital offense in the old Greek culture, so his captain and fellow soldiers brought him before Alexander. "He's a good man—he's just young," they said. "His father has served you faithfully. Please pardon him."

They had won the battle, so the commander showed mercy. The grateful lad was leaving when Alexander the Great asked, "By the way, what is your name?"

The young soldier replied, "My name, sir, is Alexander."

The commander went into a fit of rage. He raced to the fellow and shook him hard and said, "Young man, either change your ways or change your name!"

The punch-line catches you by surprise. Your guide goes on to explain how, just like today, people of that time would name their sons after great leaders because they wanted to honor what the statesmen or soldier had done. But for the next few minutes, your mind wanders away from the talk about Hellenistic culture as you contemplate your tour guide's story.

How often do we do this kind of thing today? you wonder. *We might easily honor someone with what we say or by the name we call ourselves. But when it comes to doing a service that might cost us something (life, in this case)—well, the admiration doesn't go quite that far.* Then an unsettling thought hits you. *How often do we do that with God? Would Christ say to us, "Either change your ways or change your name"?*

It's true. Sometimes people go through all the motions on Sunday with their lips and their hands, and they seem to sport the name *Christian* quite well. But through the course of the week, if you watch the way they live, you'll notice an inconsistency. They're not serving their King, they're serving themselves. The Lord is happy when we worship him with the praise of our lips. But he also desires the service of our lives. And sometimes that means we have to sacrifice.

The Meaning of Sacrifice

Service unto the Lord is another of the ways we show God that we hold him in the highest esteem. Through various avenues of ministry we attribute worth to him. But service with the adjective *sacrificial* in front of it is the kind we want to learn about in this chapter.

Probably few North Americans have much comprehension of what a *sacrifice* really involves. Most of us haven't experienced the word in its truest sense. So let's explore what a sacrifice is, because in the Old Testament it is directly related to worship.

Sacrifice gives up something good to get something better. In our culture we usually think of sacrifice as "delayed gratification." You wait to get something until you can have what's best. You do without that trendy car until the end of the year when it goes on sale—then you can get a great car for a great price. You scrupulously save your money by putting it into an I.R.A. Though you might miss out on a few "extras" now, you won't be in want when you retire. You give up something good to gain something more valuable. That's not too painful, as long as your goal's worth the wait.

In baseball, if you have a runner on first, and you need a run, you bunt. That's called a sacrifice: it means you give up an out for the sake of moving the runner into scoring position. Or, if Ryne Sandberg is at bat with a runner on third, and the

Cubs have just one out in the inning, the coach will signal the batter to hit a long fly. The man on third base will be able to tag up after the catch and score before the outfielder can throw the ball to the catcher. That's called a sacrifice fly. Again, you sacrifice an out for the thing you really need—a run that will tie or win the game. A sacrifice doesn't lower the player's batting average, and it can improve his runs batted in total. So it's a relatively painless action.

But a real sacrifice is a shocking concept. We accept the word *sacrifice* as part of our everyday vocabulary, yet if we ever saw an actual sacrifice, we would probably be utterly horrified.

According to Homer's epics, when the Greeks sacrificed an animal to the Olympian gods, the procedure went something like this:

> After the washing of hands, grain was scattered about; then the animal's head was drawn back so as to face upward, its throat was slit and afterward it was flayed. Slices from the thighs wrapped in fat were burned on the altar amid libations [liquid religious offerings] of red wine. (*Pictorial Encyclopedia of the Bible*, vol. 5 [Grand Rapids: Zondervan, 1976], p. 199)

If you try picturing that in your mind, you might get a little sick. A bleating sheep, a sharp knife, a slicing of the jugular, a rush of warm blood, a last feeble movement, a sudden release of life, a stripping of skin from muscle, a blending of blood and red wine sopped up by grain ... thanks, but no thanks! It's appallingly uncomfortable. It's so far removed from the feeling we usually have when we're worshipping. We'd rather think of sacrifice in our easy baseball terms.

But to a holy God, sin is abominable—it totally separates us from him. It takes something remarkably costly to reconcile us to his purity—something as precious as life. "The wages of sin is death" (Romans 6:23). That's a divine law, one that has been in operation since the beginning. We need to understand that, or else we won't understand sacrifice. This is the reason the lives of countless animals were taken in ancient Israel.

In the New Testament, God went one giant step further. He sent his Son as the ultimate sacrifice of love. When Christ died for us, that was the final, costly payment for sin. Nothing more is needed to reconcile us to God. But what an incredible sacrifice for the Lord to make! That's a huge reason for us to laud him as people of praise; it's what we point to in awe as people of the Christ event; that's why, as people of celebration, we get so excited. Christ died for us, but he came to life again, victorious over sin and death.

And that's why we gladly give ourselves to him as people of service.

A Living Sacrifice

"I urge you," writes St. Paul in Romans 12:11, "in view of God's mercy, to offer your bodies as living sacrifices, holy and pleasing to God—this is your spiritual act of worship."

Wait a minute. If Christ paid the final price to reconcile us to God, why this talk about *us* doing the sacrificing? And what is a *living* sacrifice? It sounds like an oxymoron.

You know what an oxymoron is. It's a figure of speech in which contradictory terms are placed side by side so that if you take them literally, they don't make much sense. It's the combination that gives them special meaning. Some folks would say postal service is an oxymoron because you don't get very good service in a post office. We don't know if that's fair, but we could cite other examples—common expressions like jumbo shrimp, or deafening silence, or pretty ugly, or fairly biased, or . . . living sacrifice.

Even in a living sacrifice, something has to die. In baseball, a sacrifice means an out—a little death, perhaps, but a death of that batter's opportunity at the plate. In a living sacrifice, it's not an animal that perishes; instead, our will dies. When we offer ourselves to God as a sacrifice, we offer to do his will instead of ours. Most Americans hold their freedom of choice as something so precious that they'd almost rather be shot than give it up. So it does end up being a kind of death on our part. We give up something good—our own will—for something better—God's will.

What is God's will? The writer of Hebrews declares doing good and sharing with others are sacrifices that please God (Heb. 13:16). That sounds like what Jesus said. He wants us to do unto others as we would have them do unto us. He wants us to be servants. This isn't usually what we want to do.

The difficulty is that being servants requires a certain death to self.

Now that can be painful.

We must learn to serve others as we would serve the King. To make things easier, the Lord lets us in on a secret. As people of service, when we reach out to others in love, it's as though we are ministering to the King himself.

This doesn't just relate to jobs within the church. In New Testament times, the Greco-Roman culture permitted slavery. A slave was in a position of constant service. (In fact, his or her vocation *was* to serve . . . and serve . . . and serve.) It got tiresome, as you can imagine. Ephesians 6:5-7 has some encouraging words for Christian slaves, and we should pay close attention to them:

> Slaves, obey your earthly masters with respect and fear, and with sincerity of heart, just as you would obey Christ. Obey them not only to win their favor when their eye is on you, but like slaves of Christ, doing the will of God from your heart. Serve wholeheartedly, as if you were serving the Lord, not men . . .

We need to take the same attitude in our jobs and in other instances when we are called upon to serve. We ought to respect our bosses, be honest and straightforward, and *always* work to the best of our ability. That's because we're employed in the business of God, not just the business of washing windows, or keeping a client's accounting straight, or selling cosmetics, or fixing someone's car. When we work as if we're doing the job for the Lord, it brings him glory. And of course, it raises our service to a whole new level.

God is pleased when we serve others. Let's look again at a verse we mentioned earlier: Hebrews 13:15-16, which reads, "Through Jesus, therefore, let us continually offer to God a sacrifice of praise— the fruit of lips that confess his name. And do not forget to do good and to share with others, for with such sacrifices God is pleased." We praise God with our lips, and the outcome of that is (or should be) our actions. Doing good and sharing with others is a sacrifice that pleases the Lord.

My (David's) wife loves it when I say to her, "What can I do for you?" The other Saturday Karen was sick. When I asked her if there was anything I could do, she responded, "I guess I could use a little pampering."

So I fixed breakfast in bed for her and then went out and bought some cut flowers. I arranged them in two vases, which I placed in the bedroom so she could enjoy them. I also got her a Saturday paper and some Diet 7-Up. And she was so impressed, I'm afraid she's going to want to get sick again!

But by my service I demonstrated that she is special to me. It made her feel important and appreciated. My service let her know I love her. The same thing is true in our relationship with the Lord. We attribute worth to him by saying, "What can I do that would please you?" And it pleases him when we serve the people he loves.

When our lives are living sacrifices, we attribute worth to God. Contemplate Paul's words: "Offer your bodies as living sacrifices ... *this is your spiritual act of worship"* (italics ours). You may never have considered service as worship. But it is. It's as much a way of attributing worth to God as singing a praise chorus. And just as with your praise, your desire in serving doesn't call attention to yourself, but to the Lord. When we serve, we're not hoping people will look at our lives and think great things about us. What we want is for others to look at our lives and think great things about *God.* It's really that simple.

A sacrifice of service also brings glory to God by helping us to appreciate what he's done in our behalf. As we read the Old Testament we notice God saying, "Always bring the best. I don't want a lamb that's not worth much to you. I want the finest of the flock."

He doesn't ask for our best simply because that shows he's most important to us. He hopes we will bring him our most precious gift because that is what he gave to us. When he asks for our best he says, "You have to understand, that's what I gave. When I sacrificed my Lamb, it was the most valuable possession I had to offer."

That's why we give him the most precious thing we can—our entire lives. It's kind of like the "Hokey Pokey": you put your whole self in. We serve him with all we have to offer, not just the parts we don't particularly care about or want or need. That helps us understand God's heart, his extravagance in giving his only Son. And when we understand how extreme his sacrifice was, we can't help but appreciate him. It only increases our worship of the King and makes us want to serve him all the more.

Serving Sacrificially: Going to Extremes

How often do we go to the extremes we would if we saw Jesus receiving our service? If Jesus were sitting at your table arrayed in all his glory, you wouldn't just serve him a meal—you'd put on the finest banquet you could. You wouldn't squeeze a dollar into his palm—you'd go to the bank and get as much money as you had for him. You wouldn't offer to do one project for him—you'd devote your whole life to helping him all you could.

It's impossible to go to those extremes for each person in the world. But we can go to extremes for certain ones God places in our path. How?

We can give extreme monetary gifts. I (Laurie) have to tell you something about David. (He'd never reveal this about himself, so I'm going to do it!) David is the most generous man I have ever known. Last Christmas the rest of us in the Mains family decided to "pay him back" for all the past years when he'd given to us so lavishly. We said to his face that we were just going to give stocking-stuffers, instead of regular presents (as the family grows, it gets increasingly hard to finance Christmas gifts). Then we all went out and secretly bought the best gifts we could for him.

The crazy thing is, he still out-gave all of us. We were so excited about the "mound of gifts" we had for him, but when we looked at the things he had given the rest of us, his pile didn't look quite as big as we'd thought it would!

That's just the way David is. He is constantly giving—not just to his family members, but to everyone. When he finds out someone needs something, he tries to meet that need. He doesn't always take credit for it; often it's a secret gift (I know he does that because he taught his son, my husband, to do it, too). But one of his greatest joys in life seems to come from giving to others.

Now, I know very well that David doesn't have very much spare money. He works for a nonprofit ministry, so he doesn't have a big salary, and he ends up giving a lot of what he does earn back to The Chapel. Sometimes—especially after income tax time—I'm pretty sure he doesn't have a penny left in his bank account! But he always manages to find a way to give to those who have even less than he does. I've never seen anything like it.

That's why David's my role model for sacrificial giving. He gives to others with the mindset that he is giving to God. What a way to attribute worth to his King! He says he learned how to give that way from his father. And now he's passing the principle (so to speak) on to his children—I want to follow in his footsteps because he reminds me of Jesus.

When I write about giving extreme financial gifts as an act of worship, that doesn't mean I think you should pop a thousand dollars into every beggar's hand. Rather, I'd like to suggest that you give just beyond what's easy for you. (If a thousand dollars here or there is just beyond your comfort zone, I'd love to be in your position!) That sacrificial giving is a beautiful example of service. And it's an act of worship that truly pleases God.

We can sacrifice by being extremely kind to others. Some folks just have the ability to make people feel good. Maybe you can remember a teacher or a coach who really knew how to build your self esteem when you were younger. Maybe someone in your church always reaches out an empathetic hand when you need it. Those are the people you tend to remember—they're the ones who empower you, even when you don't necessarily deserve that kind of encouragement. The apostle Paul is a good example of one who was especially kind.

Paul led a young slave to the Lord, which wasn't such an uncommon incident, except that this particular slave, Onesimus, had stolen money and run away from home. What's more, he'd done this terrible thing to Paul's friend Philemon, a leader in the Colossian church.

Paul could easily have simply reprimanded Onesimus and sent him back to face the discipline he deserved. But he didn't; he showed extreme kindness instead. Paul not only befriended the runaway slave; he became so close to him that he called Onesimus his son. (See Philemon 10.) And when at last he sent the young man back to his owner, Paul asked that he be treated as courteously as Philemon would treat the apostle himself. Furthermore, he offered to pay back out of his own pocket anything that Onesimus might owe his master after what he had done.

Think how good Onesimus must have felt. Formerly he would have been too afraid to go back home, but Paul's letter of recommendation encouraged him both to return to his master and to be an ideal worker for him. That's extreme kindness. It must have brought God such glory in Philemon's household.

When we make a habit of being kind to others—even when they don't deserve it—we serve them. We do this because we know we're really worshipping the King. And he deserves it!

We can serve to the extreme by selflessly contributing our talents. My (Laurie's) mother is a great example of someone who uses her gifts to serve the Lord. I know Mom would never admit to being a notably skilled musician, but she does have talent and years of training—and she uses what God has given her to go above and beyond the call of duty in serving him.

I don't remember a time in my life when Mom wasn't involved in using her music for the Lord. From singing in the adult choir to directing children's choirs (which, believe me, can be a sacrifice!) to playing the piano for Sunday morning (and evening, and Wednesday night . . .) worship, my mother has continually given her musical gifts to serve the Lord and his people. I've never heard her say, as I might be inclined, "There are many people more talented than I am. I'm sure God would rather have their gifts. Maybe I won't play for the service today." Mom has helped to bring people delight, and she's enabled them to enter God's throne room. It's all a part of how she worships. She goes to the extreme to serve her King.

Do you have a certain ability you could give to God? Maybe you're good at reading aloud, or cooking, or decorating, or figuring out finances. How can you dedicate those gifts to serving the Lord and his people? And then, how can you go to the extreme in that service?

We can give to the extreme within our family. Sometimes it's hardest to be a servant to those within our family, and we agree that sacrificial giving in our home is a must. But we want to set before you the example of some who have gone even further in their giving.

Maybe you've read about couples who have adopted underprivileged children from other countries. Taking in orphans and giving them not only a home, but a family, is a beautiful sacrifice of service to God.

I (Laurie) worked with severely handicapped children for a few summers while I was in college. Many deformed children live in State or county institutions because their parents don't want to take care of them. Some of those kids are entirely abandoned. But as I worked with the children, I became aware that certain families that *did* take care of their kids went to wonderful extremes in their care. Some of them weren't even the original parents; they had adopted the handicapped children. I believe they served those special youngsters with a love that could only be attributed to God. These acts of worship must have made a huge impression on others. I know they deeply influenced me.

If you have an opportunity to serve by taking someone into your home—or by caring in a special way for one of your own family members—God is pleased when you go to sacrificial extremes in those situations. It may not seem like much of an "opportunity" to you at the time, but serving within the family is an admirable way to worship the Lord.

We can go to extremes in being hospitable to people who can't return the favor. In the movie *Babette's Feast*, a young woman who has been forced to escape France finds work in Denmark as a cook with two elderly, godly sisters. Babette's only link to her home country is a lottery ticket, and after having served the sisters for more than a year, she finds out she has won ten thousand francs.

She asks her employers to allow her to prepare a feast for their church members. You see, she had previously been a great French chef of whom it was said, "This woman, this head chef, had the ability to transform a dinner into a... love affair that made no distinction between bodily appetite and spiritual appetite."

Babette serves the simple townsfolk a lavish feast—the finest meal they've ever eaten. And it does seem to nourish their spirits as well as their bodies. Though they had been bickering and back-biting in past meetings, the people find that the meal miraculously promotes good will among them.

Babette explains it with these simple words: "I was able to make them happy when I gave of my very best."

After they find out the exhausted Babette has spent her entire fortune on the meal, the two sisters are flabbergasted. "In Paradise," sister Phillipa says, "you will be the great artist that God meant you to be. Ah, how you will delight the angels!"

We believe that the moment you bring others into your home and give them your best, you delight the angels—and the King of Kings. That gift of your most precious service is extreme hospitality. And it brings great glory to God.

We can go to the extreme in giving precious time. This could be the hardest thing for some of us to do. The older we grow, the less time we have to live and do our own thing, so time can become all the more costly in our minds.

My (Laurie's) father has been a minister since I was twelve, and even before that he was extremely involved in church leadership and in counseling those who were troubled. Any minister is called upon to give many hours to the service of his flock. But I have seen Dad donating what most would consider huge amounts of time to people outside the church, to community functions, and to churches that were not directly under his care.

I have vivid memories of going to a nursing home with my dad on Sunday afternoons. We would spend time with the elderly people there, and Daddy would lead them in a church service. I can't figure out how he had time to teach Sunday school, direct

Christian education, and assist the senior pastor in our large church; come home and eat a big meal with the family; run across several suburbs to hold church for the old folks; and finally, go back and help to officiate a Sunday evening church service. It seemed impossible—but he did it!

Now that we three kids are out of the house, Dad and Mom invite to their home other young people who might not have good family relationships or who just could use someone to talk to. And even though he holds down a full-time job, plus an interim pastorate, plus a church sectional leadership position, Dad manages to find time to spend with those who need him.

Still, throughout the years I lived at home, I don't ever remember feeling like Daddy didn't have time for me. He was there when *I* needed him, too. I'm convinced he did it all as a service to the Lord.

Try giving some time to serving people in your church, your community, a nearby school, a special outreach, or anywhere else you feel God wants you to go. We're convinced you'll find great delight in sacrificing your time for others. And we know God will be overjoyed.

There are many other ways we can serve others as we would serve our King. Maybe the best way for you to worship the Lord is by saying, "What are the most precious things I can offer?" and then giving those to someone else. This not only pleases the Lord; it is a genuine act of worshipping God.

Are you beginning to realize that worship is a huge topic? If we've communicated that idea, we've accomplished one of our purposes in writing this book. Not that we have covered the subject adequately; we've barely scratched the surface. But it's important for worship to be seen as more than praise.

Yes, praise is a great beginning place. And if it were the whole of worship, praise would still be a study too great for any of us to master. But praise is only an entry point to the exploration of worship.

We also wanted to give you a new perspective on important areas of life that, for whatever reason, have become common or mundane. If you've learned to look at your whole life in a new way as an act of worship, we've accomplished another of our goals.

That fresh perspective on worship is one benefit you'll discover as you consciously center your life on Christ. Your joy in that new outlook spills right over into celebration as you learn to delight in the presence of the Lord. And your delight and desire to honor him will result in diligent service for his sake. They all tie together as marvelous tools for attributing worth to God.

The truth is that worship is life-encompassing. If we were experts (which we're not), even in a book ten times this size we wouldn't be able to do much more than write a simple introduction to how we can put God in his rightful place in our lives. Maybe it's a good thing we're still learning in this area—we can still relate to most of our readers!

Imagine once again that you are in a museum. It doesn't have to be a museum of ancient history this time, but picture yourself in a large one, like the Smithsonian in Washington, D.C., or the Museum of Science and Industry in Chicago, or maybe (if you're really an adventurer) the Louvre in Paris. Suppose you're a visitor in town, and you only have a couple hours to spend in one of these places. But you're determined to see *everything*.

You'll soon figure out it doesn't work that way. In all the aisles and wings and sections and buildings of the vast museum, there are just too many wonderfully diverting, mind-stretching things to see! After a while, all you can do is say, "I'm going to view what I can and enjoy that. Then, I'll just have to come back and visit this place again, because it's simply incredible."

The two of us feel like tour guides pointing out some of the highlights of a "worship museum," knowing fully well we can't do justice to the whole. But we want you to realize that you've started to explore something far better than what you might have expected. We hope this short visit to the vast treasury of worship will bring you back, resolved to pursue it further. And if you ever run into us, we're hoping you'll say, "David! Laurie! I'm so excited—I'm learning all kinds of fascinating truths about putting God in his place. I don't know when I've ever enjoyed my relationship with the King more!"

If you say that, our eyes will shine and our hearts will swell—we'll be absolutely thrilled. And we'll have just one thing to tell you:

It only gets better.

For Discussion and Reflection

1. Recount a time when someone sacrificed to help you.

2. How have you served the Lord in the past? Did you think of this as worship? Why or why not?

3. Explain what St. Paul's term "living sacrifice" means to you.

4. In what specific circumstance do you feel you truly sacrificed to serve the Lord?

5. Name something precious that God might someday ask you to use in his service.

6. After reading this book, what kinds of changes would you like to make in your worship of the King?

Readings

The point that we must always keep before us is that worship has a horizontal as well as a vertical dimension. It is important for us to enact the work of Christ as an offering of praise and thanksgiving to the Father. But it is equally important that we *act on* what we have enacted. If we really praise God for the redemption of the world through Jesus Christ, then we must do as Paul instructs: "Offer your bodies as living sacrifices, holy and pleasing to God—which is your spiritual worship. Do not conform any longer to the pattern of the world, but be transformed by the renewing of your mind" (Rom. 12:1-2). The pattern of this world is one of injustice, inequality, discrimination, war, hate, immorality, and all those human abuses that the New Testament and early church fathers describe as the way of death (see Rom. 1:21-32; Gal. 5:19-21; Col. 3:5-9; *Didache*, 5-6). The true worship of God inevitably leads the people of God into positive social action. Our calling is to worship God not only with our lips but with our lives.

(Robert E. Webber, *Worship Old and New* [Grand Rapids: Zondervan, 1982], p. 190)

••••••

Paul minces no words: "Therefore, I urge you, brothers, in view of God's mercy, to offer your bodies *as living sacrifices,* holy and pleasing to God—which is your spiritual worship" (Rom. 12:1, emphasis added).

Perhaps the most difficult pill to swallow, especially for Americans, is the thought of giving without obligating a reciprocal benefit from the receiver. We frequently trade favors in business and neighborhood life. We offer help with the implied understanding that the person will do the same for us when we need it. That's not bad, either!

It's just not how lifestyle worship works. With God, if we give in order to get, then we give amiss. We are then thinking of ourselves first and of God second—a dangerous order of priorities.

Lifestyle worship will benefit us, but it is not primarily for our benefit. If our focus is ultimately on ourselves, then we fall into the witless trap of worshiping a compromised creation instead of our incomparable Creator. Such truncated vision will produce personal barrenness.

Lifestyle worship is sacrificial. A sacrifice is a gift of the essence or the product of our lives. It may be a gift of our time, a gift of our talent, or a gift of our treasure. Whatever shape it takes, it is a sacrifice given with no regard for a return on that investment.

Mary's sacrifice was time. She devoted a portion of this irretrievable commodity to sitting at the feet of Christ instead of spending it on His meal. This, in turn, sacrificed peace in the household as Martha vented her anxiety in the presence of all her guests.

Hannah sacrificed the momentary pleasure of personal revenge on her rival, leaving that instead to God. She also sacrificed her treasure, Samuel, giving him up as a child to full-time, lifetime temple ministry rather than keeping him at home where she could see, care for, and enjoy her son as other moms did their children.

Paul sacrificed health, wealth, marriage, comfort, and prestige in order to devote himself to the mission of bringing the Gospel to the Gentiles of his generation. All of us who are Gentiles today can thank him for his faithfulness to that calling.

The sacrifices we may offer through lifestyle worship are not unnoticed by God. He sees them all, and He will not let them go unrewarded. In fact, our giving garners greater gain!

Be patient, though. Temporal life is a blink compared to eternity, when our true gains are realized. Consider Moses:

"By faith Moses, when he had grown up, refused to be known as the son of Pharaoh's daughter. He chose to be mistreated along with the people of God rather than to enjoy the pleasures of sin [e.g., the luxury and prestige in Egypt's royal palace] for a short time. He regarded disgrace for the sake of Christ as of greater value than the treasures of Egypt, because he was looking ahead to his reward" (Heb. 11:24-26).

(John Garmo, *Lifestyle Worship: How to Bring Worship into Your Daily Life* [Nashville: Thomas Nelson Publishers, 1993], pp. 66–68)

●●●●●●

First, the Old Testament word *hishahawah* means literally "a bowing down" and emphasizes the way in which an Israelite fittingly thought of his approach to the holy presence of God. He bows himself down in lowly reverence and prostration. The term indeed is used of men's homage to their fellows who, as V.I.P.s, commanded respect, . . . but the full significance is seen in the use of the word when it means the Hebrew's approach to God, the great King and sovereign Lord. . . . The Greek term, used in the Septuagint to translate *shahaah,* is *proskunein,* with the same overtone of submissive lowliness and deep respect.

The second term is *'abodah,* translated "service." It is from the same root that the term *'slave', 'servant'* (*'ebed*) is taken; and this is important. For the highest designation of the Hebrew in his engagement with the worship of God is just this word *'servant'.* He delighted to call himself God's *'ebed* . . . and expressed that joy in his acts of private and corporate praise and prayer. Unlike the Greek thought of slavery as servile abasement and captivity, the Hebrew notion, implicit in the word *'ebed,* expressed the relationship of servant and kindly master. . . . This bond was thought of and described in terms of privilege and honour more than of inhuman bondage; and when men called themselves 'the *servants of God'* in the cultic sense, they were paying tribute to the intimate and honoured relationship into which God had brought them. Thus, Israel's great leaders are so called *the servants of God* (especially David). . . . The corresponding Greek term is *latreia* (service); and in the light of the background in the Old Testament, we should understand Paul's use of the same Greek word. . . . He sees it as his and the Church's solemn privilege and honour to be entrusted with the service of the Gospel. That service is his offering to God of that worth and honour by which He is glorified in the salvation of the Gentiles.

(Ralph P. Martin, *Worship in the Early Church* [Grand Rapids: Eerdmans, 1974], pp. 11–12)

●●●●●●

One of my African students at Regent College moved into a housing complex in suburban Vancouver and recorded his experience of culture shock in moving to urban Canada. In his home country, Tanzania, when a family moves into an area it is big news. People visit them, and they are expected to visit their neighbors without any prior notice. As they walk to the open market, to their place of work, or the community well, they invariably will meet people along the way and speak with them. "In this place," Justyn Aforo noted, "people have cars and they can even get into their cars without stepping out of the house. People know one another and recognize each other on the street by the cars they drive and the jobs they do." The Aforos were deeply lonely and felt unwelcome. But rather than yield to despair, Justyn and his wife decided to show hospitality to the people who should have been their hosts. Though they were busy, full-time students and parents, they reached out to welcome their neighbors by celebrating the birthdays of neighboring children, having coffee times with the mothers, sponsoring community dinners, and developing a prayer fellowship for the few believers they discovered in their complex. *Hospitality* in the Greek language literally means love for the stranger. But in this case the stranger did the loving. . . .

Tragically, the stranger often turns out to be a member of our own church, a workmate on the job, a next-door neighbor, or even a member of our own family. So hospitality is not a leisure-time hobby or an avocational interest. It is part of our continuous ministry of living for God seven days a week. The stranger in our lives is an invitation to relate to God—a spiritual discipline. And responding to our neighbor in love is a ministry.

(R. Paul Stevens, *Disciplines of the Hungry Heart* [Wheaton, Ill.: Harold Shaw, 1993], pp. 167–168. Used by permission.)

● ● ● ● ● ●

Endow the king with your justice, O God,
   the royal son with your righteousness.
He will judge your people in righteousness,
   your afflicted ones with justice.
The mountains will bring prosperity to the
   people, the hills the fruit of righteousness.
He will defend the afflicted among the
   people and save the children of the needy;
   he will crush the oppressor.

He will endure as long as the sun,
   as long as the moon, through all
   generations.
He will be like rain falling on a mown
field, like showers watering the earth.
In his days the righteous will flourish;
   prosperity will abound till the moon

is no more....

For he will deliver the needy who cry out,
  the afflicted who have no one to help.
He will take pity on the weak and the
  needy and save the needy from death.
He will rescue them from oppression and
  violence, for precious is their blood in
  his sight....

All nations will be blessed through him,
  and they will call him blessed.

Praise be to the LORD God,
  the God of Israel,
  who alone does marvelous deeds.
Praise be to his glorious name forever;
  may the whole earth be filled with his
  glory.
Amen and Amen.
(from Psalm 72)